SAMS
Teach Yourself

the Internet

by Galen Grimes
with Rick Bolton

in 10 Minutes

SAMS

A Division of Macmillan Computer Publishing
201 West 103rd St., Indianapolis, Indiana 46290 USA

To my older brothers Rod and Brod, who helped me find so much about life as we were growing up. I hope this helps them find the Internet.

©1998 by Sams Publishing

International Standard Book Number: 0-672-31320-0
Library of Congress Catalog Card Number: 98-84597

99 98   8 7 6 5 4 3

Interpretation of the printing code: the rightmost number of the first series of numbers is the year of the book's printing; the rightmost number of the second series of numbers is the number of the book's printing. For example, a printing code of 98-1 shows that the first printing of the book occurred in 1998.

Screen reproductions in this book were created by means of the program Collage Plus from Inner Media, Inc., Hollis, NH.

Printed in the United States of America

Publisher John Pierce

Managing Editor Thomas F. Hayes

Acquisitions Director Cheryl D. Willoughby

Production Editor Kate Givens

Technical Editors John Purdum, Brian Hubbard

Editorial Assistant Jennifer L. Chisolm

Book Designer Kim Scott

Cover Designer Dan Armstrong

Production Team Marcia Deboy, Maribeth Echard, Trey Frank, Christy Lemasters, Sossity Smith

Indexer Craig Small

WE'D LIKE TO HEAR FROM YOU!

Sams has a long-standing reputation for high-quality books and products. To ensure your continued satisfaction, we also understand the importance of customer service and support.

TECH SUPPORT

If you need assistance with the information in this book or with a CD/disk accompanying the book, please access Macmillan Computer Publishing's online Knowledge Base at **http://www.superlibrary.com/general/ support**. If you do not find the answer to your questions on our Web site, you may contact Macmillan Technical Support by phone at **317/581-3833** or via e-mail at **support@mcp.com**.

ORDERS, CATALOGS, AND CUSTOMER SERVICE

To order other Sams or Macmillan Computer Publishing books, catalogs, or products, please contact our Customer Service Department at 800/428-5331 or fax us at **800/835-3202** (International Fax: **317/228-4400**). Or visit our online bookstore at **http://www.mcp.com/**.

COMMENTS AND SUGGESTIONS

We want you to let us know what you like or dislike most about this book or other Sams products. Your comments will help us to continue publishing the best books available on computer topics in today's market.

> Sams
> 201 West 103rd Street
> Indianapolis, Indiana 46290 USA
> Fax: 317/581-4663

Please be sure to include the book's title and author as well as your name and phone or fax number. We will carefully review your comments and share them with the author. Please note that due to the high volume of mail we receive, we may not be able to reply to every message.

Thank you for choosing Sams!

CONTENTS

Introduction

Do you know where you can find:

- The current U.S. census?

- The FBI's Ten Most Wanted list?

- Schedules for all NCAA Division I football and basketball games?

- Pictures of Mt. Everest and Mt. K2?

- Information on certain types and brands of inline skates?

- A list of movies that are playing in your city this weekend?

- The number of Cokes left in the soda machine on the 7th floor of Watson at Columbia University?

- The answer to the question "Which actors have portrayed Romulans on Star Trek: The Next Generation?"

- A list of research studies that have been conducted on asthma in the past 10 years?

- The price of the Doors CD *Morrison Hotel?*

If you haven't guessed by now, the answer is that you can find all of these things on the Internet—without ever leaving the comfort of your favorite chair.

In the past few years, the Internet has experienced phenomenal growth, not only in the amount of information and services that are available online, but also in the number of people accessing that information. However, there's more to the Internet than just information, facts, and figures. The Internet has been invaded by entertainment promoters and entrepreneurs. Hundreds of businesses are now investigating ways of advertising their names and products online because of the potential audience they can reach.

Today, just about everyone wants to get on board the Internet express. Only a few years ago, it seemed like you would need a doctoral degree in computer science to figure out the vagaries of connecting to the Internet. You had to know UNIX and how to set up and configure TCP/IP protocol stacks, SLIP/PPP connections, and IP addresses. Thank goodness those days are long gone.

WELCOME TO SAMS' TEACH YOURSELF THE INTERNET!

Teach Yourself the Internet in 10 Minutes takes a straightforward, easy-to-understand approach to guiding you through every aspect of setting up your PC and connection, getting you connected to the Internet, and then showing you what you can do once you get there.

Teach Yourself the Internet in 10 Minutes is for anyone interested in...

- Understanding how to establish an Internet account.

- Using a Windows or Mac platform to access and discover the Internet.

- Learning what a Web browser is and how to use one to access the most popular branch of the Internet: the World Wide Web.

- Locating information and entertainment on the World Wide Web.

HOW TO USE THIS BOOK

In addition to teaching you how to connect to the Internet, this book gives you a broad range of helpful information about the Internet. You will learn how to explore the Internet and how to use the Internet as a valuable research and information source.

You can use this book as a handy resource. Keep it close to your PC even after you have finished reading it cover-to-cover. If you keep this book handy, as you venture into new areas of the Internet, you can use it to discover how to make use of those new areas.

CONVENTIONS USED IN THIS BOOK

You'll find the following icons throughout this book. They mark information intended to help you save time and to teach you important information fast.

 Timesaver Tips icons indicate inside hints for using the Internet more efficiently.

 Plain English icons call your attention to definitions of new terms.

 Panic Button icons mark warnings and cautions about potential problem areas.

You'll also find the following conventions used throughout the book to help you know what you're supposed to do:

What you type	Things you need to type appear in bold type.
Press Enter	Keys you press, buttons you click, and items you select appear in blue type.
On-screen text	On-screen messages appear in bold type.

Press Alt+F1   Key combinations you must press simultaneously appear in this format. This means that you press and hold the first key (in this case, the Alt key) and then press the second key (F1). Then you release both keys.

TRADEMARKS

All terms mentioned in this book that are known to be trademarks have been appropriately capitalized. Sams cannot attest to the accuracy of this information. Use of a term in this book should not be regarded as affecting the validity of any trademark or service mark.

ACKNOWLEDGMENTS

Special thanks to Macmillan's book-building team: Jill Byus, Stephanie Gould, Henly Wolin, Martha O'Sullivan, Kate Givens, Lori Cates, Audra Gable, San Dee Phillips, and all the folks in Proofreading and Layout. None of this would have been possible without their long hours and patience with me.

FINDING OUT ABOUT THE INTERNET AND THE WORLD WIDE WEB

In this lesson, you learn what the Internet is, how the World Wide Web is a part of the Internet, and why so many people are attracted to both of them.

WHAT IS THE INTERNET?

If you've watched the news much in the past year or two, undoubtedly, you've noticed all the hoopla over the Internet. Although the Internet, or its forerunner ARPAnet, has been around since the late 1960s, you would think that the worldwide network of computers magically became connected during the last two years. The Internet has been the hot topic lately, and it doesn't seem likely that the topic will cool down in the near future.

The Internet's popularity has fueled the demand for books such as this one, designed to help ease you into what, at first, must seem like a technological hodgepodge. The Internet may seem insurmountable. By the time you finish this book, however, you'll think of yourself as an Internet expert. You'll understand Web browsers and TCP/IP stacks, as well as FTP sites and PPP connections, and you will likely be showing other, less-informed users how to access search engines and FTP servers.

Access to the Internet is, foremost, access to a wealth of information, from academic research to stock market quotes (see Figure 1.1) to information on hang gliding and inline skating (see Figure

1.2). You can do geographical and geological research, and you can even review Casey Kasem's weekly Top 40 hits list (see Figure 1.3).

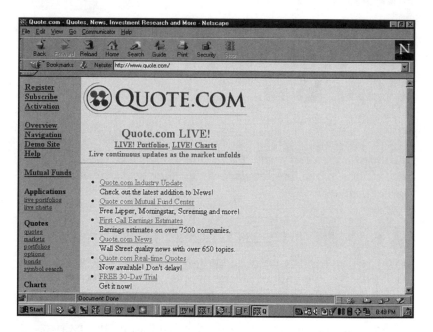

FIGURE 1.1   The Quote.Com financial service provides current stock quotes.

Originally designed as an academic-exchange medium, the Internet has become a favorite target of burgeoning entrepreneurs who sell everything from stocks, bonds, and mutual funds to compact discs, music boxes, and vintage wines.

The Internet's access and appeal have also naturally caught the attention of most major computer hardware and software manu-facturers and vendors. They've found that the Internet, or "the Net," is an excellent way to reach and provide information and upgrades to their customer base and potential customer base. Besides Intel (whose home page is shown in Figure 1.4), other well-known computer vendors with a presence on the Net include IBM, Compaq, Novell, Apple, and, of course, Microsoft.

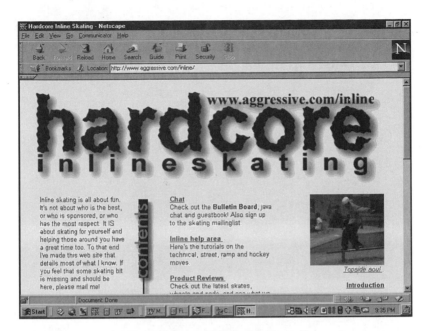

FIGURE 1.2   Check out inline skating on the Web.

FIGURE 1.3   Casey's Top 40.

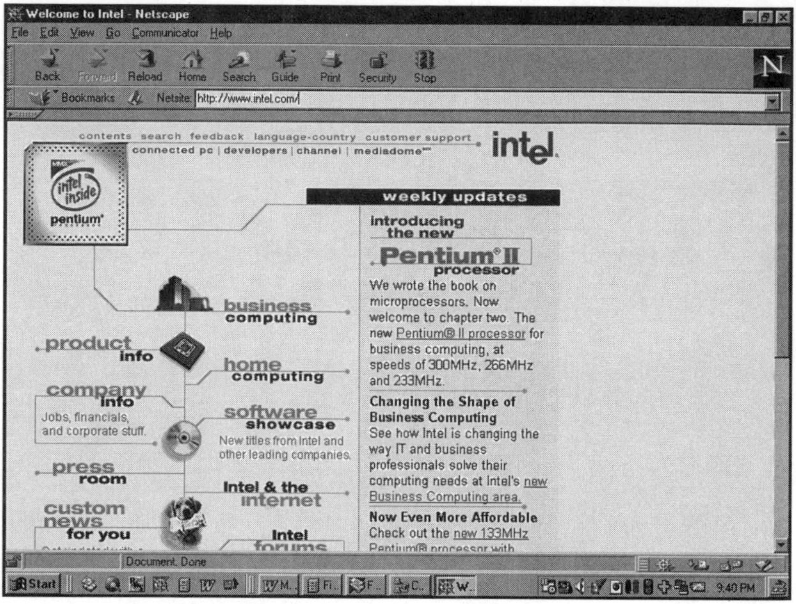

FIGURE 1.4   Intel's Home Page.

PIECES OF THE INTERNET: HOW THEY FIT TOGETHER

The Internet is a worldwide series of interconnected computer systems and a series of several different types of computer services. While many of you might already be fairly familiar with the World Wide Web, you may be less familiar with Gophers, newsgroups, or FTP sites. The following sections outline some of the more popular services available on the Internet.

E-MAIL

E-mail is the oldest Internet service, dating back to the mid 1970s (the exact date of the first e-mail message is in dispute). Then and now, the basic concept behind e-mail is fairly simple: You log in to a computer system and write and address a text message to a user on another system. The message is then routed through the maze of interconnected computer systems until it is delivered to its intended destination.

While the concept might be the same, the e-mail products you use now (see Figure 1.5) bear little resemblance to the early e-mail systems of the '70s and '80s.

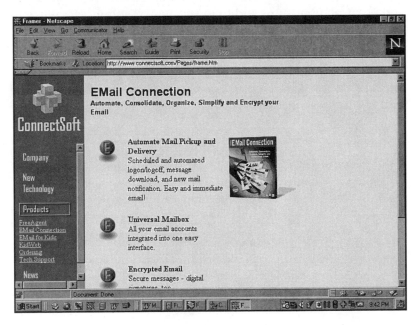

Figure 1.5 Email Connection, an Internet e-mail program.

E-mail still allows you to send text messages, but you can also attach other types of files, and encrypt messages to prevent anyone but the intended recipient from reading it. There are even free e-mail-only services you can subscribe to if your only interest in the Internet is e-mail. Lesson 13 explains more about sending and receiving e-mail messages.

UseNet

UseNet refers to a service somewhat similar to e-mail, except that instead of sending a message to one person, you post the message in a common area for many users to view and reply to. UseNet began in 1979 as a service connecting computers at Duke University and the University of North Carolina. Today, UseNet is an immensely popular Internet service that has grown to include more than 4,000 topics that users post messages and responses to, ranging from computer and technical topics to social, religious, and political discussions and to music, books, and movies. Figure 1.6 shows a screen from a newsreader program, which you use to access UseNet.

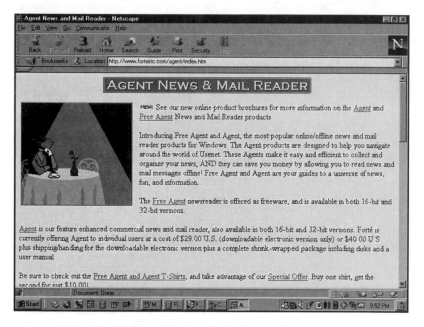

FIGURE 1.6   Forté Agent, a popular newsreader.

Newsgroups can also be a good source of information from other users who have used certain products, have seen certain movies or shows, or have had experiences with certain companies.

If you think you might be interested in joining or participating in a newsgroup (or two or three), check out Lesson 15. It explains how to find them and how to join in on the discussion.

FTP

FTP (File Transfer Protocol) refers to both an Internet service and a UNIX utility (it's also now a Windows 95 utility). The Internet service FTP is a series of computer file servers that archive and distribute files. Many FTP sites are operated by computer hardware and software manufacturers who use their FTP sites to distribute their software and software updates. Netscape, one of the major Internet Web browser companies, uses its FTP site to distribute its Web browser, Netscape Navigator.

FTP sites are also run by colleges and universities that use them to make shareware and software utilities available to a broad range of users. Lesson 14 gives you the lowdown on accessing FTP sites.

CHAT

IRC (Internet Relay Chat) is another immensely popular Internet service. As the name implies, IRC is a system that allows users to congregate in a common area, in this case, an IRC server, and chat with each other. It's not vocal chat, though—you communicate by typing your contribution to the conversation. Whereas a year or two ago chat rooms comprised a totally separate service on the Internet, now chat rooms are starting to crop up on the Web.

Don't expect to find too many highbrow discussions among Rhodes scholars and rocket scientists in IRC. A considerable percentage of the discussion groups (called chat rooms) center around popular and adult topics. However, occasionally, when there is a hot topic in the news, you might find several newsgroups that banter the subject around. If you are interested in engaging in chat room discussions, be sure to review Lesson 17.

THE WORLD WIDE WEB

Even though the World Wide Web, often referred to simply as the Web, is the newest service on the Internet, it is without a doubt the most popular. The Web went online in 1992, a creation of Tim Berners-Lee of CERN, the European laboratory for Particle Physics in Geneva, Switzerland. By October of 1993, there were more than 200 Web servers up and running, and by June, 1995, the total number of Web servers on the Internet totaled more than 6.5 million.

Part of the Web's attraction is the fact that it is the only multi-media service on the Internet. The Web began as a text-only system, as did FTP, Gopher, and e-mail. The Web now is a cacophony of text, graphics, sounds, animation, and virtual reality.

The Web also seems to have no boundaries for the type of information you can find on Web sites. A lot of it may seem to be trivial, but Fortune 500 companies have been attracted to the Web in droves, and slowly part of the Web is becoming the cyber marketplace of the '90s.

You can also find information from or about:

- Government agencies (federal, state, and local)
- Colleges and universities
- Professional and amateur sports teams
- Political organizations
- Social and cultural organizations
- Health and science
- Computer hardware and software manufacturers
- Business opportunities on the Web

In this lesson, you learned what the Internet is and why it is so popular. In the next lesson, you will find a detailed examination of the hardware and software you need to access the Internet.

HARDWARE AND SOFTWARE YOU WILL NEED TO ACCESS THE WEB

In this lesson, you learn about the equipment and programs you need in order to access the World Wide Web.

THE HARDWARE YOU'LL NEED

While it is possible to access the World Wide Web with any computer that will run Windows 3.1 (which includes a 386 with as little as 2–4 megabytes of memory), you'll need a fairly powerful system to take full advantage of what the Web has to offer. A practical minimum configuration for using Windows 3.1 or Windows 95 is a 486/25 with 4–8 megabytes of memory (RAM). Unless you plan to download a tremendous volume of files, your hard disk requirements do not need to be gargantuan; a minimum hard disk of 120 megabytes is more than sufficient. You will need VGA graphics, and while you can get by with a video card that supports only 16 colors (if you like viewing what appear to be "washed-out" graphics, or opt to use a text-only Web browser), most of the graphics you will encounter will look a lot better with a video card that supports 256 colors.

And last but not least, you will need a modem to navigate the Web. The minimum speed for a modem you should even consider is 14,400 bits per second (bps). (A 9,600bps modem isn't just sluggish, it is down right torturous.)

Now, if you want to get past a "minimum" configuration and start looking at a more realistic configuration, start with at least a 486/50 with 8–12 megabytes of memory, a 400 megabyte hard disk, a video card with 1 megabyte of video RAM (which will support 256 colors with no problem), and a 14,400–28,800bps modem.

Another item you will want to invest in is a sound card. Much of the Web now boasts multimedia extensions, most notably sound, and you will need a sound card as well as speakers or a headphone to hear Web-based audio. If you also plan to experiment with any of the Web-based telephony products, you will also need a microphone.

Lastly, you will want to consider adding a CD-ROM drive. While a CD-ROM drive is not essential for accessing the Web, you will find that a lot of commercial software is now being distributed on CD instead of floppy disks.

After you get your hardware assembled, you'll be ready to tackle the Internet and the World Wide Web. This book helps you access the Internet directly through an Internet service provider (ISP), not through a local area network (LAN) that has an Internet gateway. For information on configuring an Internet connection through a LAN, talk to your local system administrator. For information about connecting to the Internet through an online service such as The Microsoft Network or America Online, see Lesson 23.

 Gateway   A means of "passing through" or "connecting to" a system different from the one you are using. An Internet gateway for a local area network is merely a means of providing Internet access to users on a LAN.

You need an Internet account with an Internet service provider (ISP). If you don't have an Internet account yet, see Lesson 19, which explains how to select an ISP.

You also need a means of communicating with your service provider. This book assumes that your connection is over a standard
telephone line using a modem. For acceptable performance, as
stated earlier, you will need a modem capable of communicating
at a rate of at least 14,400bps. People often refer to these modems
as "14.4" (fourteen-dot-four) or "V.42" (vee-dot-forty-two). A
slower modem doesn't provide an acceptable performance level
for accessing graphical images over the Internet. A 33.6/28.8 modem gives the best performance over standard phone lines.

> **V.34**   The international specification for 33.6/28.8 (asyn-
> chronous) modem communications. Communications
> organizations from all over the world meet on a regular
> basis to decide communications specifications. These
> specifications dictate how hardware devices are to per-
> form when communicating certain types of signals at
> certain speeds. The specification for 14.4 modem com-
> munications is V.42.

Another communication technology that looks to have a big im-
pact on Internet usage is ISDN. ISDN (Integrated Services Digital
Network) is literally "digital telephones." Rather than convert
your computer's digital signals into analog (sound waves) to be
transmitted over standard telephone lines as a modem does, ISDN
transmits a digital signal over digital telephone lines. The advantage is a communication connection up to 128 kilobits per second
(kbps) as opposed to today's 28.8kbps connections. In many parts
of the country, ISDN is available in roughly 70–90 percent of the
local Baby Bells' service areas.

In addition to its lack of availability, the downsides to using ISDN
lie in the difficulty of locating a knowledgeable telephone company sales office, and in its cost. Many regional telephone sales
offices will still respond "...ISD-what?" And when you do find
service in your area, pricing is still geared more towards businesses
than consumers. But don't despair. ISDN pricing is going down
and availability is still improving.

Even if you do find a local Bell office knowledgeable enough
about ISDN to be able to place your order, the installation of ISDN
can still be a formidable task. While the phone company might be
able to successfully run the line to your computer, getting the
ISDN adapter (contrary to what you've heard, there is no such
thing as an "ISDN modem") properly configured and working will
still largely be your responsibility (or your problem depending on
how you want to look at it). But most ISDN adapter vendors have
now made it easier than ever to get ISDN service working in your
home. (I made the move to ISDN last year and it was not as pain-
ful as I had imagined.)

Another connection option that is getting lots of headlines but
that is still moving at a snail's pace is the "cable modem." Instead
of getting service through your telephone company, you would
connect to the Internet through your cable TV provider. Getting
the proper equipment in place by the providers is still the largest
roadblock. Most of the current cable TV system is still designed as
a one-way system (they provide service to you). To convert to a
two-way service, fiber-optics cables need to be installed along
with the necessary routing communications equipment. If
Internet service demand continues at its present rate, meaning
that there is still a strong profit motive in providing Internet access, cable modems in most of the country are still 18 months to
two years away for most of us.

THE SOFTWARE YOU'LL NEED

Obviously, you need an operating system with a graphical user
interface such as Windows 95, Windows NT, Mac System 7.5.x, or
X/Windows installed on your computer to get the most out of
this book and the Internet. You can connect using Windows 3.1,
but there is a big push towards 32-bit software because of its im-
proved performance, which means 95 or NT.

While a graphical user interface (GUI) is not essential for Internet
access, you will probably be spending a large percentage of your
time browsing the World Wide Web. And although you can view
the Web in a text-only mode, the view is considerably better if

you include the pictures and colors, which necessitates a GUI-based operating system.

You will also need software. Windows 95 and Windows NT provide all the software you need to connect to the Internet, as do most flavors of UNIX that support X/Windows. If you are using an Apple Macintosh, there are several good Internet access packages you can purchase rather cheaply that can get you up and running in no time.

The primary tool you will use to access the information on the Web is a browser. Lessons 4 through 9 explain some of the basics of the two most popular browsers: Netscape Navigator and Microsoft Internet Explorer.

WINDOWS 95 INTERNET SOFTWARE

If you are running Windows 95, you may have heard that you need the Windows 95 bonus package, Microsoft Plus!, to gain Internet access. Microsoft Plus! provides a collection of additional utilities and programs for Windows 95, including the Internet Setup Wizard. The Internet Setup Wizard makes it easier to connect to the Internet, but it is not essential. Lessons 19, 20, 21, and 22 explain how to connect to the Internet, both with and without Microsoft Plus!.

If you're not sure if all or part of Microsoft Plus! has been installed on your computer, follow these steps to find out:

1. Select the Start button on the taskbar and choose Programs, Windows Explorer.

2. On your C:\ drive, locate a folder labeled Plus!. If you don't see this folder, it's likely that none of Microsoft Plus! has been installed on your PC (or at least on your C:\ drive; if you have more than one drive, check the others, too). If you do see the Plus! folder, check to see if the Internet Tools have been installed in a folder called Microsoft Internet. You can still get Internet access with a package available from Microsoft called "the Internet Jumpstart Kit."

3. Open the Start menu and choose Programs, Accessories. If
   your Accessories menu contains an Internet Tools option,
   choose Internet Tools to see if you have the Internet
   Setup Wizard installed (see Figure 2.1).

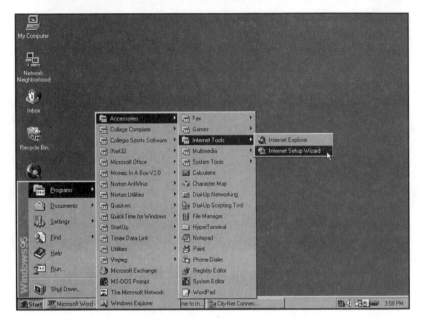

FIGURE 2.1   The Internet Setup Wizard is installed.

WINDOWS 3.1 INTERNET SOFTWARE

A good percentage of the packaged Internet access software is
designed for Windows 95, but there is still plenty to choose from
that will operate on the Windows 3.1 platform. However, you can
save a few dollars by checking with your service provider for it.
Most Internet service providers will include software and instructions on how to set up your system at no extra charge.

For More Information on Configuration... If you need assistance installing and configuring your Internet connection software, skip ahead to Lessons 19, 20, 21, and 22, which provide detailed instructions for configuring Internet software on Windows 3.1 and Macintosh platforms.

In this lesson, you learned about the hardware and software you need to get up and running on the Web. In the next lesson, you will learn how to use the first of two Web browsers covered in this book: Microsoft's Internet Explorer.

Using Microsoft Internet Explorer

In this lesson you learn to use the Microsoft Internet Explorer 4.0 Web browser.

Microsoft's Internet Explorer

Microsoft released Windows 95 with Internet support and several Internet utilities. In Lessons 6, 7, and 8, you will learn about the Web's most popular Web browser, Netscape Navigator, the major application in the Netscape Communicator suite. In this lesson, you learn about Microsoft's Web browser, Internet Explorer 4.0 (IE4)—Microsoft's latest release of its Web browser product. Compare the two Web browsers to see which one you prefer.

Internet Explorer was originally available only for Windows 95, but now Microsoft releases versions that will run under Windows NT, the Apple Macintosh, and on selected UNIX platforms.

Before you can use Internet Explorer 4.0, you need to get a copy and install it. If you purchased the Windows 95 add-on product, Microsoft Plus!, you already have a copy of an earlier version of Internet Explorer, version 2.0, which you can use to download IE4. If you used the Microsoft Plus! Internet Setup Wizard (also called the Internet Jumpstart Kit) to set up your connection to your service provider, you also have the earlier version of Internet Explorer (version 2.0) already installed. If you started out with Internet Explorer 2.0 and later upgraded to IE3.0, that's okay, too. IE3 will work just as well as IE2.

If you purchased your computer with Windows 95 preinstalled, check it for software; some dealers have included the Internet

Jumpstart Kit as a bonus. If you're not sure if this bonus was included with your system, ask your dealer.

To get your copy of Internet Explorer 4.0, follow these steps:

1. Start Internet Explorer 2.0. In the Location text box, enter the URL **http://www.microsoft.com/ie/ default.asp**, and the Microsoft Internet Explorer Web page appears (see Figure 3.1).

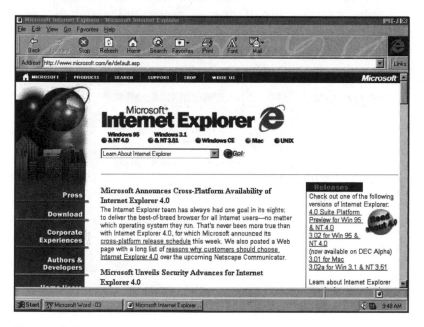

FIGURE 3.1   The Microsoft Internet Explorer Web page.

2. Select the Download link on this page (it should be on the left side but it might have been moved). Follow the instructions to download the version of the Internet Explorer 4.0 setup program that runs on your PC.

   In previous versions of Internet Explorer, you would download the entire program and then install the program on your computer. Now Microsoft has you download a setup program and then you run the setup program to install IE4.

This change makes it easier for the user, since IE4 can be installed in four different configurations. By using the setup program to install IE4, you will only download the parts of the program you actually need for the configuration you choose.

3. When the download is complete, copy the downloaded file to its own directory. Then run the setup program to install IE4. Microsoft recommends (and I concur) that you should first just install the basic or standard version of IE4 (see Figure 3.2), and if later you want to upgrade to one of the enhanced versions, you can run the setup program again.

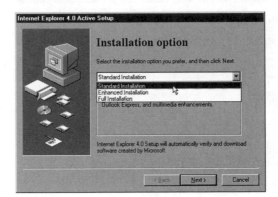

FIGURE 3.2   The four installation choices for IE4.

USING IE4 AS YOUR WEB BROWSER

Let's go ahead and start the program so you can begin getting familiar with IE4.

To start IE4:

1. Double-click the Internet Explorer icon on your desktop to start IE4. When Internet Explorer starts, it automatically loads the Internet Explorer 4.0 Home Page which is part of the Microsoft Web site (see Figure 3.3).

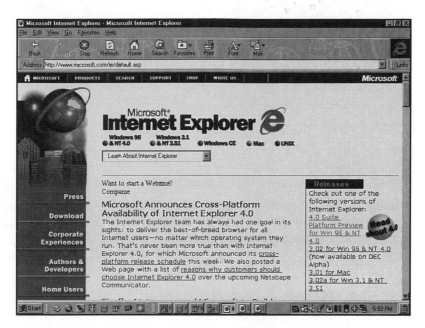

FIGURE 3.3   The Microsoft Internet Explorer 4.0 Home Page.

2. Explore the Internet Explorer Web site by jumping to some of the other links on this page— and on the home page of the Microsoft Web site at **http:// www.microsoft.com/**.

3. To jump to a new Web site, open the File menu and choose Open. Enter the following URL in the Open dialog box:

   http://www.hbo.com

   This URL takes you to HBO's Home Page on the Web, where you can view and listen to several interesting pages.

HBO Didn't Appear! Some URLs are case-sensitive, so you must make sure you type every URL exactly as it is shown here. If you typed http://www.HBO.com, for example, you might not get HBO's Web page. Also note that the characters following http: are forward slashes (//), not backslashes (\\).

INTERNET EXPLORER'S TOOLBAR

Notice the toolbar across the top of Internet Explorer's screen. It contains 10 icons that are preprogrammed to perform some of the most commonly used commands. Table 3.1 explains each icon's purpose.

TABLE 3.1   INTERNET EXPLORER TOOLBAR ICONS

ICON	NAME	DESCRIPTION
Back	Back	Takes you to the preceding page.
Forward	Forward	Takes you to the next page. (This only works if there is a next page you've previously viewed.)
Stop	Stop	Stops a graphic from loading to the currently viewed page or stops the current page from loading.
Refresh	Refresh	Reloads the current page and its graphics.
Home	Home	Reloads the Internet Explorer's home page, or whatever home page you've specified.
Search	Search	Takes you to a search page on Microsoft's Web site where you can use various Internet search engines.

continues

TABLE 3.1   CONTINUED

ICON	NAME	DESCRIPTION
Search	Favorites	Opens the folder (window) containing your Favorite Page shortcuts.
Print	Print	Prints the currently displayed page.
Font	Font	Allows you to change the fonts displayed on Web pages.
Mail	Mail	Starts your designated e-mail client or MS Exchange.
Edit	Edit	Gives you the same options as the Edit menu.

Don't worry if you are not totally familiar with each icon on the toolbar. In later lessons you will learn what each icon is used for.

In this lesson, you learned about Microsoft's Internet Explorer Web browser—how to get it and install it, and how to use it. In the next lesson, you learn how to place markers on certain Web pages you visit with Internet Explorer so you can easily return to them.

MARKING FAVORITE PAGES IN INTERNET EXPLORER

In this lesson, you learn how to use Internet Explorer's Favorite Pages feature to keep track of Web pages you've visited.

RECORDING YOUR FAVORITE PAGES

Microsoft Internet Explorer gives you a means of recording Web sites you've visited. Some Web browsers refer to these records as bookmarks. In Internet Explorer these records are Favorite Pages.

To see how the Favorite Pages feature works, follow these steps:

1. Open the File menu and choose Open. The Open Internet Address dialog box appears. Enter the URL **http://www.nfl.com** and click OK. In a few seconds, you should be at the home page of the National Football League.

> **Enter the URL Directly** If you don't like having to open the Open Internet Address dialog box every time you want to enter an URL, you can type the URL directly into Internet Explorer's Address box to save time.

2. Open the Favorites menu and choose Add To Favorites, and the Add To Favorites window shown in Figure 4.1 appears. Click the OK button to add the current page to your list of favorites.

FIGURE 4.1 Add the current page to your Favorite Pages list.

3. Back in the main Internet Explorer window, open the Favorites menu again. Now you see that a shortcut to this Web page is listed there (see Figure 4.2).

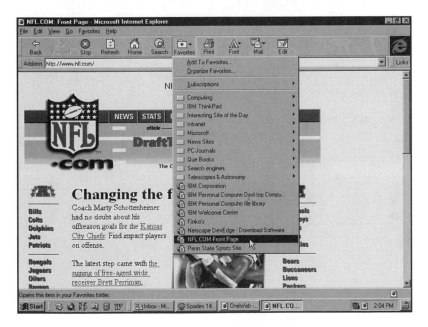

FIGURE 4.2 The Favorites menu contains shortcuts to your favorite pages.

ORGANIZING FAVORITE PAGES SHORTCUTS

If you haven't guessed by now, Favorite Pages are really Windows 95 shortcuts, created inside a special folder called Favorites, which is created in your Windows folder. Because they are shortcuts in a folder, you can manipulate them the same way you would manipulate any other group of shortcuts in a folder.

Here's how you can organize your shortcuts:

1. Jump to **http://espnet.sportszone.com** and add it to your Favorite Pages folder.

2. Select Favorites, Organize Favorites to open the Organize Favorites dialog box.

3. Click the New Folder button to create a new folder.

4. Type Sports as the folder name.

5. Drag the Team NFL and the ESPNET SportsZone shortcuts into the Sports folder (see Figure 4.3).

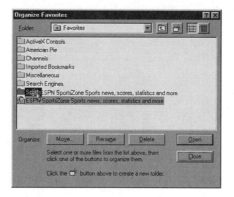

FIGURE 4.3   Dragging the ESPN Favorite into the Sports folder.

6. Close Favorites, and you return to the main Internet Explorer window.

7. Open the Favorites menu. In place of the two shortcuts
   you created earlier, you'll see the Sports folder. Click the
   Sports folder to see your two shortcuts (see Figure 4.4).

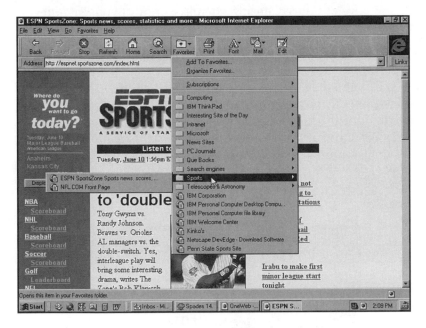

FIGURE 4.4   Shortcuts arranged in a folder.

You can use this technique to create category folders for the Favorite Pages shortcuts you create, so you can group them together
and find them easier. Keep in mind that you can always delete
folders and favorites you no longer need as another means of
organizing your Favorites and keeping them from getting clut-
tered.

> **Change of Appearance**   You can open the Favorites
> menu (select Favorites, Organize Favorites), and select
> the folder you want to change. Then choose Open Favor-
> ites and change the appearance of your Internet Explorer
> shortcuts using the View menu option just as you would to
> change any folder full of icons (to change large icons to a
> text listing, for example).

PUTTING FAVORITES ON YOUR DESKTOP

If you haven't noticed already, there is a copy of your Favorites menu on your desktop already. In Windows 95 and NT, Internet Explorer 4 places a copy of your Favorites menu into your Start menu.

You can also drag individual Favorite Pages shortcuts to your desktop the same as you would any other shortcut icon. If there are favorite places you regularly visit, you might find it helpful to drag the shortcuts to your desktop where they are more accessible. To drag a shortcut to your desktop, follow these steps:

1. Resize your IE window to make it look like the one in Figure 4.5.

FIGURE 4.5   A resized IE4 window.

2. Select Favorites, Organize Favorites, and then open the Sports folder (see Figure 4.6).

FIGURE 4.6   Open the Favorites folder and the Sports folder.

3. Right-click and drag the desired shortcut from the Favorites folder to your desktop.

4. In the shortcut menu that appears, select either Copy Here or Move Here to move or copy the shortcut to the desktop. (If you select Move Here, you will remove the original shortcut from the Favorites folder.)

In this lesson, you learned how to make records of favorite Web sites you visit using Internet Explorer's Favorite Pages feature. In the next lesson, you will learn how to subscribe to Web sites for downloading and offline viewing.

BROWSING OFFLINE AND SUBSCRIBING TO PAGES

In this lesson, you learn how to subscribe to a Web site and download selected pages for offline viewing.

VIEWING WEB PAGES OFFLINE

A new feature added to IE4 is the ability to download all or portions of a Web site to your computer so you can view the contents of the Web site offline. *Subscribing* and *offline viewing* are mainly used for sites you visit on a regular basis.

The advantages of offline viewing are that you can view the Web site at your leisure, you don't have to wait for each page to download and be displayed, and you have an organized copy of the site and the pages you want to view. The major disadvantages to offline viewing are the amount of disk space you can potentially use in storing a copy of a Web site and the amount of time involved in downloading the site to your computer. Both of these listed disadvantages can be controlled however, as you will soon see.

Rather than spending a lot of time explaining how subscriptions work, you will probably understand the function better if I simply demonstrate how it's done:

1. Jump to the Web site or page you want to subscribe to. For this example let's go to the MSNBC Web site at **http://www.msnbc.com**.

2. Select the Favorites menu, then choose Subscriptions, and then select Subscribe to open the Subscription dialog box (see Figure 5.1).

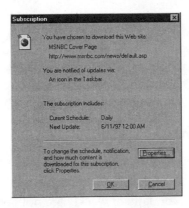

FIGURE 5.1   The Subscription dialog box.

3. At this point your subscription is entered and you can simply select OK to close the dialog box. But chances are you will want to modify the subscription parameters to better control how the subscription and download will be performed, so go ahead and select Properties to open the Properties dialog box (see Figure 5.2). The Properties dialog box allows you to change the settings for how often the designated pages are downloaded to your computer, how many pages are downloaded, and how you will be notified of changes in the subscribed Web site.

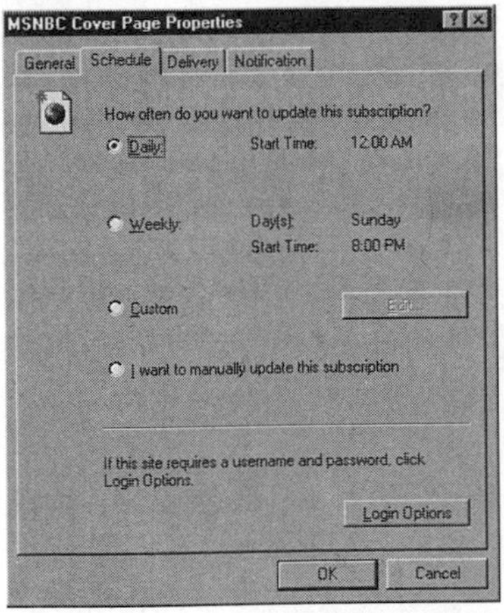

FIGURE 5.2   The Subscriptions Properties dialog box.

CHANGING THE UPDATE SCHEDULE

The default setting for delivery of the pages you will have down-loaded is daily starting at 12:00 A.M. You can change the delivery schedule to Weekly (meaning you will only get downloaded pages once per week), custom (meaning you can set whatever delivery schedule you desire), or manual (meaning no delivery will take place until you initiate the update).

If you change the delivery schedule setting to weekly, your update will take place starting Sunday morning at 8:00 P.M.

If the preset times for daily or weekly are not convenient, you can set the schedule to Custom and then set the delivery schedule time to whatever suits you.

To make a custom schedule change:

1. Make sure the Schedule sheet in the properties dialog box is displayed by selecting the Schedule tab.

2. Select the Custom option button.

3. Select the Edit button to open the Custom Schedule dialog box (see Figure 5.3).

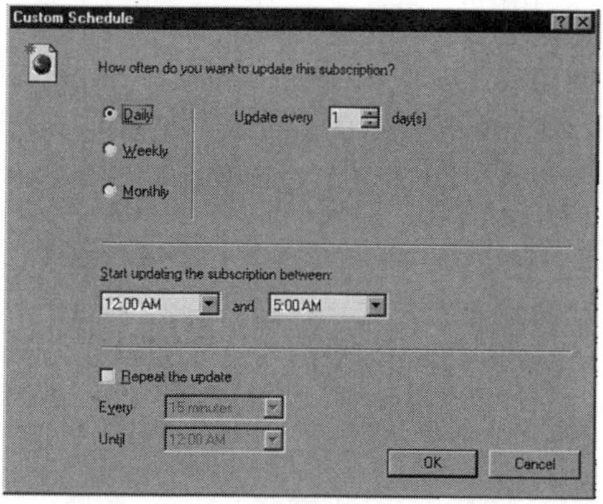

FIGURE 5.3   The Custom Schedule dialog box.

4. If you select the Daily option button you can specify that the update occur every day, or arbitrarily set the day counter. In this context, Daily specifies that the time between updates will be counted by days (as opposed to being counted by weeks or months). For example, you can specify Daily, and then set the update counter for every 5 days. The range of the counter is 1–1000 days.

5. If you select the Weekly option button (see Figure 5.4) then you can specify selected days of the week that you want the update to occur and you can specify the weekly increment for the update. For example, if you want a particular site updated every other Tuesday and Thursday you would select the Tuesday and Thursday check boxes and set the update counter to update every 2 weeks. The range of the counter is 1–1000 weeks.

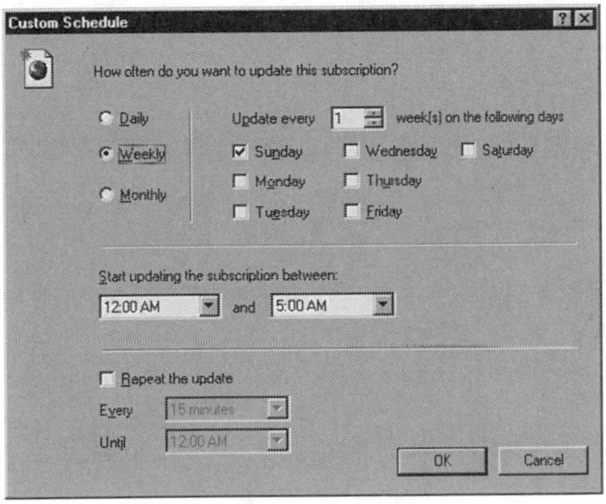

FIGURE 5.4   You can set your subscription to update weekly.

6. If you select monthly as your update frequency (see Figure 5.5), which can be somewhat confusing, you can then select to have your subscription updated on day 1–1000 of every 1–1000 months, or you can select the {first, second, third, fourth} {Sunday, Monday, Tuesday, Wednesday, ... Saturday} of every 1–1000 months.

7. After you select the update frequency (daily, weekly, or monthly), then you can select the update time. For the update time you specify a range of time in which the update(s) will be performed. The range can be between 12:00 A.M. and 11:30 P.M. in 30 minute increments.

> **Don't Be Alarmed by the Available Range!** Just because days and months have a range of 1–1000, don't think you really need to be concerned about how far 1000 days or 1000 months can be. Just use 1–31 as your range for days and 1–12 as your range for months. If you need to extend days beyond 31, use one more month. If you need to extend months by more than 12 (though I can't imagine anything that you would ever need to update with a frequency greater than once every 12 months), simply use one more year.

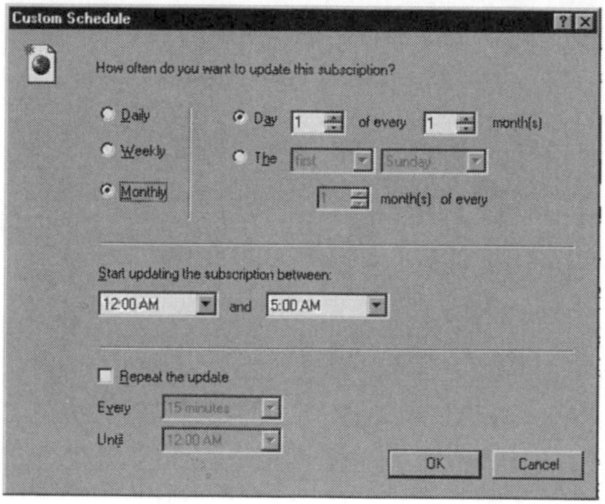

Figure 5.5 You can set your subscription to update monthly.

8. And lastly, you can specify that the update be repeated. The repeat increment can be set from every 15 minutes— 12 hours between 12:00 A.M. until 11:30 P.M.

9. To complete and save your Custom schedule, select OK.

CHANGING THE QUANTITY OF DELIVERED PAGES

Whenever you subscribe to a Web site, one of the most important settings you can configure is the "quantity of delivery;" literally, how much of the Web site you want downloaded to your computer. Unfortunately, this is not always a highly quantifiable setting. If you set the quantity too low, you risk wasting time and not getting enough of the information you want. Set the quantity too high and you tie up your computer and your Internet connection in a long download and waste precious space on your hard disk. It all boils down to whether you like to play it safe, or whether you are willing to take a risk!

To set the delivery quantity for your subscription:

1. Make sure the Delivery sheet in the properties dialog box is displayed by selecting the Delivery tab (see Figure 5.6).

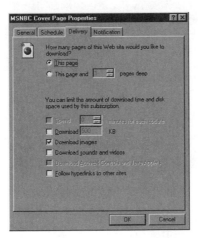

FIGURE 5.6   The Delivery sheet in the Properties dialog box.

2. You first need to determine how many pages you want to download. You can select just the first page of the subscribed Web site or you can select the top page and 1–1000 pages on the Web site

3. To hedge your bets on how much text and images you will be downloading, you can set limits on how much time is spent performing the update (in minutes) and a limit on the how much (in kilobytes) you download to your computer's hard disk. You can also specify whether images will be included in the update, along with sound and videos, ActiveX controls and Java applets, and most importantly whether links will be followed to other Web sites.

Be Security Aware—Not paranoid! ActiveX control and Java applets can potentially expose you to serious security risks since they can be made to damage your files by unscrupulous computer hackers. You should exercise extreme caution in allowing Java applets and ActiveX controls to be downloaded to your computer. If you are subscribing to any sites from companies or individuals you are not familiar with you may want to forgo downloading ActiveX controls and Java applets.

Don't Download Everything! You might also want to exercise caution when allowing downloads to follow links to other sites. This option can also potentially inflate the size of your updates.

4. To complete and save the Delivery settings in your update select OK.

SETTING YOUR NOTIFICATION OPTIONS

You've seen how IE4 gives you a lot of latitude in deciding how often you want to have your subscriptions updated, but remember at any time you can manually update your subscriptions from the Favorites menu. To help you decide if you want or need to perform a manual update (or adjust your update schedule), IE4 allows you to set a notification option which will let you know when any of the sites you have subscribed to have changed. You can set IE4 to notify you either by setting an icon on the taskbar or by e-mail.

To set your notification options:

1. Make sure the Notification sheet in the Properties dialog box is displayed by selecting the Notification tab.

2. You can select to display the update icon on the taskbar and/or to have IE4 notify you by e-mail. To select to display the update icon select the Show notification icon on the taskbar check box.

3. To have IE4 notify you by e-mail, select the Send notification via Internet mail check box. You will also need to enter your e-mail address and the name of your outgoing e-mail server (SMTP).

 If You Need Help! To find out more about e-mail and how to configure IE4 for e-mail, turn to Lesson 12, "Sending and Receiving E-Mail".

4. To complete and save the Notification settings in your update, select OK.

PERFORMING A MANUAL UPDATE

You can perform a manual update of your subscriptions anytime you want.

1. On the Favorites menu, select Subscriptions, View All to open the Subscriptions dialog box (see Figure 5.7).

2. Select the subscription you want to update.

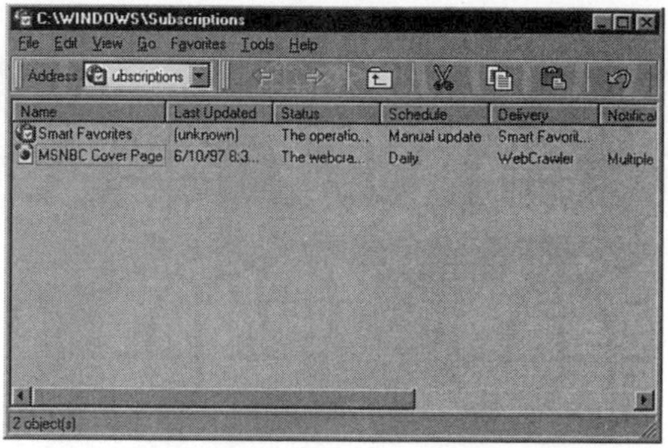

FIGURE 5.7   The Subscriptions dialog box.

3. From the File menu, select Update to begin the manual update.

VIEWING YOUR UPDATES

The last thing you need to learn about subscribing to Web sites is how to view your handiwork offline.

To view your updated subscriptions:

1. From the Favorites menu, select Subscriptions then select View All to open the subscriptions dialog box.

2. Click the subscription you want to view to display the Web site offline.

If you need to you can enlarge the subscription dialog box.

In this lesson, you learned how to subscribe to Web sites using IE4's subscription function, and how to browse your subscribed Web sites offline. In the next lesson you will learn how to search the Internet.

CONTROLLING ACTIVEX CONTROLS

*In this lesson, you learn about
ActiveX Controls and how to use them.*

WHAT IS ACTIVEX?

Quite simply, ActiveX is not a thing, but a technology. ActiveX is
a means of tying together a wide assortment of tools which enable
Web developers to create interactive Web site environments. In
this lesson you will mostly be concerned with using ActiveX controls—interactive objects in a Web page which provide interactive
controls and functioning.

ActiveX controls can be written using a variety of familiar program development tools, such as Visual Basic, Visual C++, and
Delphi just to name a few. In many ways, ActiveX controls do for
Internet Explorer what plug-ins do for Netscape—they extend the
functionality of the program. ActiveX controls also allow some
degree of interaction between you and the Web site using the
ActiveX control. Don't worry about being absolutely clear on understanding ActiveX and ActiveX controls at this point. As the
lesson progresses you should get a better feel for how ActiveX
operates.

> **Netscape Is Still not on the ActiveX Bandwagon!**
> Microsoft IE since version 2 has natively supported
> ActiveX. Netscape does not natively support ActiveX but
> there is an ActiveX plug-in you can install from **http://
> www.ncompasslabs.com/**.

INSTALLING ACTIVEX CONTROLS

One of the best places to acquire ActiveX controls is from the Microsoft ActiveX Component gallery, located on the Microsoft Web site at **http://www.microsoft.com/activex/gallery/default.htm**. To give you an example of the interactive nature of ActiveX controls, let's download and install a sample ActiveX control from Microsoft's ActiveX Component Gallery page.

1. Start IE4 and enter **http://www.microsoft.com/activex/gallery/default.htm** to go to the Microsoft ActiveX Component Gallery page (see Figure 6.1).

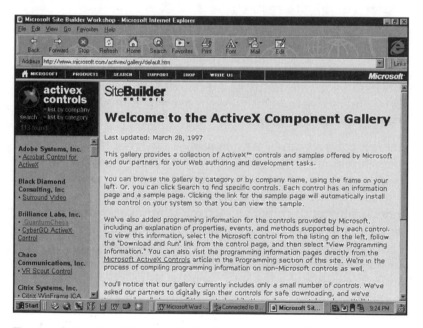

FIGURE 6.1   The Microsoft ActiveX Component Gallery page.

2. In the column on the left, select the QuantumChess link.

3. Select the link Download and run a working sample of this control. The download should go pretty quickly since the control is only 48K in size.

4. Before the download begins you will be presented with an authentication certificate (see Figure 6.2). Select Yes to approve the download.

FIGURE 6.2   An ActiveX authentication certificate.

> **Always Look for an Authentication Certificate**   Because of potential security issues involving ActiveX controls, you should never download an ActiveX control from a company that does not offer an authentication certificate guaranteeing who is responsible for creating the ActiveX control.

When the download is completed, the control will automatically load and you will be ready to play QuantumChess (see Figure 6.3).

Now that you've loaded and run the QuantumChess control, you can select Practice and play a practice game or you can select New Games, Connect to the Brilliance Labs server and play a game of chess against another Internet user.

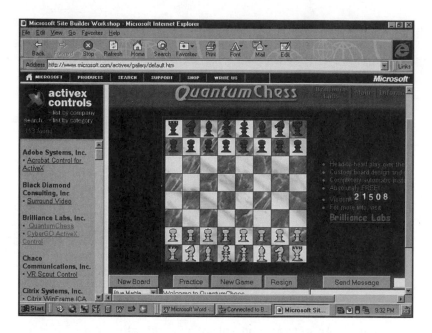

FIGURE 6.3   After the download you are now ready to play QuantumChess.

SECURITY CONCERNS WITH ACTIVEX

Downloading and installing ActiveX controls exposes you and your computer to potential security problems. ActiveX controls are small programs that you are downloading, installing, and running on your computer which come from a potentially unknown source. For this reason, most reputable ActiveX controls developers will include an authentication certificate, like the one you saw in the previous exercise to verify the creator of the control.

IE4 also has security features you can control which can give you an added layer of security.

To verify the IE4 security settings:

   1. On the View menu, select Options to open the Options dialog box.

2. Select the Security tab to display the Security sheet (see Figure 6.4). On the lower portion of this dialog box you can control how your Web browser will respond to ActiveX controls and scripts.

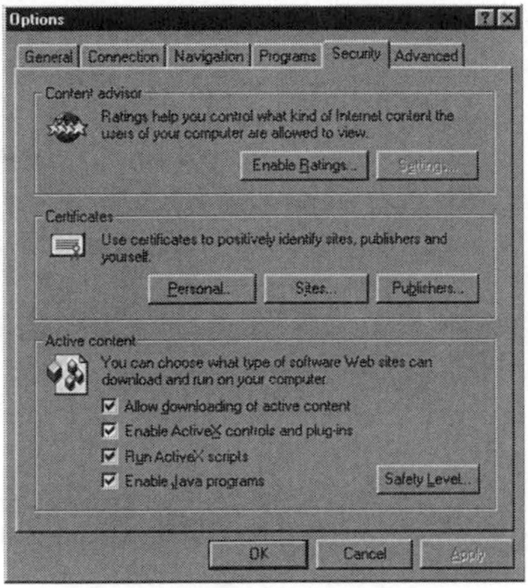

FIGURE 6.4   The Security sheet in the Options dialog box.

3. If you select Sites under Certificates, you will see a list of Certificate authorities from which IE4 is pre-configured to recognize and accept certificates.

SOME TRULY USEFUL ACTIVEX CONTROLS

If you are interested in obtaining and experimenting with (certified) ActiveX controls, here are a few places you can go to obtain more controls. You've already seen one site where you can obtain ActiveX controls—the Microsoft ActiveX Component Gallery. Another location is ActiveX.com located at **http://www.activex.com/**.

In this lesson, you learned about ActiveX and ActiveX controls and how they are used in Web page development. In the next lesson, you will learn about the Web browser Netscape Navigator.

USING NETSCAPE NAVIGATOR

In this lesson, you learn how to get, install, and use the Netscape Navigator Web browser.

DOWNLOADING AND INSTALLING NETSCAPE NAVIGATOR

One of the most popular Web browsers is Netscape Navigator, or Netscape for short. The Web browser is part of Netscape's newly released suite of Internet applications called Netscape Communicator. A *Web browser* is a special type of program that allows you to view the text and pictures contained in Web screens or, as they are called on the Web, *Web pages*. You can get a copy of Netscape by using an FTP utility to download a copy of Netscape Navigator from one of Netscape's FTP sites. If you don't have an FTP utility, you should still continue reading the remainder of this lesson, and make a note to come back to this lesson after reading Lesson 13 ("Accessing Files with FTP").

To download your copy of Netscape Communicator:

1. Start your FTP program and log in to Netscape's FTP site, **ftp.netscape.com**.

   If you are an international user, select one of Netscape's international ftp sites:

   > Stellenbosch University, South Africa: **ftp://ftp.sun.ac.za**

   > University of the Witwatersrand—SunSITE Southern Africa: **ftp://ftp.sunsite.wits.ac.za**

   > The University of Hong Kong: **ftp://ftp.hku.hk**

Hokkaido University, Japan: **ftp://ftp.eos.hokudai.ac.jp**

CAIR,KAIST (Republic of Korea): **ftp://ftp.kaist.ac.kr**

Van Nung Institute of Technology, Taiwan: **ftp://ftp.vit.edu.tw**

University of Economics, Austria: **ftp://ftp.wu-wien.ac.at**

University of Augsburg, Germany: **ftp://ftp.uni-Augsburg.DE**

Hebrew University of Jerusalem, Israel: **ftp://ftpwww.huji.ac.il**

ELETTRA, Italy: **ftp://thor.elettra.triests.it**

Type **anonymous** as your login name, and use your e-mail address as the password.

2. Once you log in to the Netscape FTP server, go to the /pub/navigator directory (or folder), select the directory containing the appropriate version of Netscape for your platform (such as Windows, Mac, or UNIX), and download the program.

3. The file you download is in an archival (compressed) format, like a ZIP file. Go ahead and extract or decompress the file's contents, copy it into a directory by itself and follow the on-screen instructions to install Netscape. If the file you download has an .EXE file extension, it is a self-extracting archive file. Just run the archive as you would any other program to decompress the archive.

> **I Have a Browser**   If you are already using a Web browser, you can probably use it to get a copy of Netscape. Enter the URL **http://home.netscape.com/try/comprod/mirror/client_download.html** and follow the links to download the Netscape browser. Note, however, that Netscape sites are often busy; the file will take 30–60 minutes to download using a 14.4 modem.

DISCOVERING THE WEB

Now that you've installed Netscape, it's time to use it to start exploring the Web.

To get to a site or page on the Web, you must tell your browser how to find that page. The Internet has devices called *FTP servers* that store files that you can download. The Internet also has devices called Web servers. These are remote computers that store the Web pages that your browser displays. The difference between a Web server and an FTP server is the way they transfer information across the Internet to your computer. An FTP server transfers files using the FTP (file transfer) protocol. Your connection to an FTP server is also continuous from the time you log on until the time you log off. A Web server sends you text and graphics, which are immediately displayed on your screen using the hypertext transfer protocol. Also, your connection to a Web server is reestablished for each page it sends you.

To start Netscape Navigator, follow these steps:

1. Double-click the Netscape icon (in the Netscape Communicator folder) to start the program. The first thing you see is the license agreement, and then you see Netscape's colorful Web page, or more precisely, its Home Page (see Figure 7.1).

> **Home Page**   The name given to the opening screen or first page of a Web site belonging to a company, group, or organization on the World Wide Web. It is analogous to a welcome screen.

2. Before proceeding, stop and take a look at the nine icons under the menu. These nine icons make up the toolbar. Most browsers have a similar set of icons. The following list tells each icon's function.

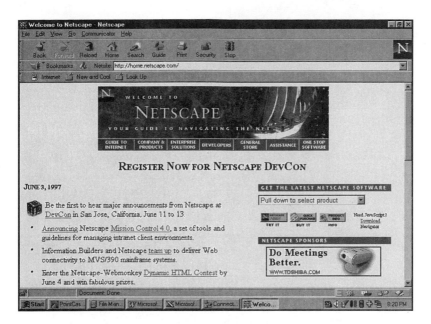

FIGURE 7.1   Netscape's Home Page.

Icon	Name	Description
	Back	This is one of the three main navigation buttons. This button is used to take you back to the previously displayed Web page in the history list. If the button is grayed out, it means you are still on, or you've returned to, your starting Web page.
	Forward	This is the second of the three main navigation buttons. This button is used to take you forward to a previously viewed Web page. If this button is grayed out, it means there is no other Web page you can go forward to get back to.

Icon	Name	Description
Reload	Reload	Redisplays the currently selected Web page.
Home	Home	This is the third of the three main navigation buttons and is used to take you back to your designated home page. By default, this is the Netscape Home Page, but you can set any page to be your home page and use this button to return to it.
Search	Search	This button is preprogrammed to connect you to a special search engine page on the Netscape Web site. Here you can conduct queries on five different Web and Internet search engines.
Guide	Guide	This button is also preprogrammed to take you to several special purpose pages on the Netscape Web site. The pages preprogrammed into this button are What's New?, What's Cool?, Destinations, People, and Software.
Print	Print	Sends the currently displayed Web page to your printer.
Security	Security	This icon now identifies the security status of the currently displayed Web page. An open lock indicates a Web page with no special security. A closed lock indicates a secure Web page.
Stop	Stop	Stops a page from loading.

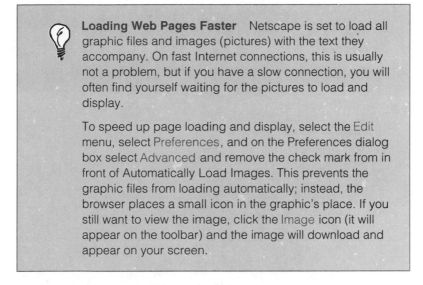

Loading Web Pages Faster Netscape is set to load all graphic files and images (pictures) with the text they accompany. On fast Internet connections, this is usually not a problem, but if you have a slow connection, you will often find yourself waiting for the pictures to load and display.

To speed up page loading and display, select the Edit menu, select Preferences, and on the Preferences dialog box select Advanced and remove the check mark from in front of Automatically Load Images. This prevents the graphic files from loading automatically; instead, the browser places a small icon in the graphic's place. If you still want to view the image, click the Image icon (it will appear on the toolbar) and the image will download and appear on your screen.

3. To go (the proper term is *jump*) to a different Web page on the Netscape menu, choose File, Open Page. The Open Page dialog box appears (see Figure 7.2).

FIGURE 7.2   Netscape's Open Page dialog box.

4. Type the URL **http://www.paramount.com** in the text box and click Open. This takes you to the Paramount Pictures home page shown in Figure 7.3.

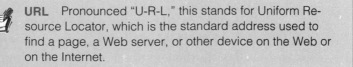

URL Pronounced "U-R-L," this stands for Uniform Resource Locator, which is the standard address used to find a page, a Web server, or other device on the Web or on the Internet.

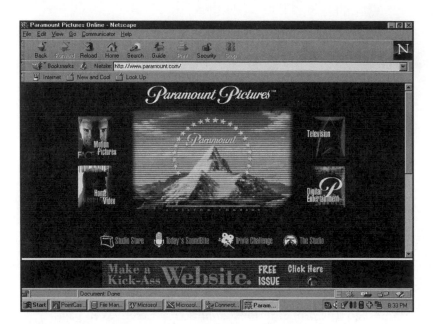

FIGURE 7.3   The Paramount Pictures Home Page.

> **Entering URLs Quickly**   You can also enter a URL in the
> Location/Netsite text box just under the toolbar. Use the
> Backspace key to delete the contents of the text box,
> enter the URL you want to jump to, and press Enter.

5. Select the Television link. On the next page select the
    Action link. Click the Star Trek: Voyager link just below
    the title. The Star Trek: Voyager Web page appears (see
    Figure 7.4).

A link connects text or pictures from one Web page to another
Web page. In a Web page, text links (made up of letters and
words) are usually shown in a different color from ordinary text
and are sometimes underlined. Links are made up of Hypertext.
Hypertext embeds links in the text that enable you to jump to
new sites and view.additional information.

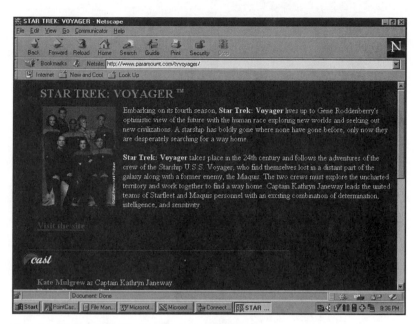

FIGURE 7.4   Star Trek: Voyager Web page.

Spend some time looking over this Web page and its links. This Web page is a good example of how text, pictures, and sound are used, and what you will see as you further explore the Web.

This Page Looks Different!   Don't panic if the home page you see for Paramount Pictures looks different than the one shown earlier. This difference illustrates an important lesson about Web pages; they change constantly. Because Paramount Pictures uses its home page to promote its movies and television shows, this page is subject to frequent change.

In this lesson, you learned about one of the most popular Web browsers, Netscape Navigator. In the next lesson, you will learn how to set bookmarks in Netscape Navigator.

SETTING BOOKMARKS IN NETSCAPE

In this lesson, you learn how to keep track of Web pages you visit using Netscape's Bookmark feature.

USING NETSCAPE'S BOOKMARKS

Over the next few months, if you spend a fair amount of time "surfin' the Net," you will likely visit hundreds of Web sites. Keeping track of the ones you want to revisit is easy if you use the built-in Bookmark feature in Netscape.

> **Bookmark** A placeholder, whether it is something you place between the pages of a book, or something you use to track pages you have visited on the Web. With Netscape, you can keep a list of these bookmarks—URLs you would like to return to.

To place a bookmark in Netscape, follow these steps:

1. Open the File menu and choose Open Page. In the Open Page dialog box, enter **http://www. planetreebok.com** and click Open. If you haven't guessed by now, this is Reebok's Home Page (see Figure 8.1).

2. Click the Bookmarks button on the Location toolbar to open the Bookmarks menu and choose Add Bookmark to place this URL in your bookmark list.

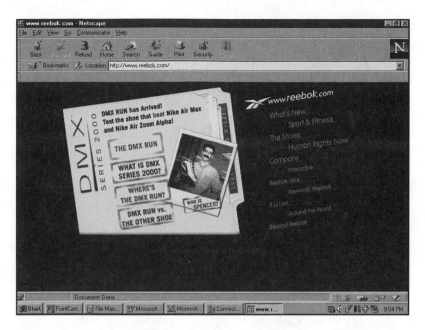

Figure 8.1   Reebok's Home Page.

Once you have marked a Web page with a bookmark, you can go back to that page at any time by opening the Bookmarks menu and then selecting the page you want to return to from your bookmark list.

Editing Bookmarks

Netscape also allows you to edit the items in your bookmark list. To do this, follow these steps:

1. Open the File menu and choose Open Page. In the Open Page dialog box, enter **http://espnet. sportszone.com** and click Open. This takes you to ESPN's Home Page. If you're any kind of sports fan, this is a good place to start on the Web (see Figure 8.2).

2. Open the Bookmarks menu again and choose Add Bookmark to place this URL in your bookmark list.

3. Open the Communicator menu and choose Bookmarks to open another view of the Netscape Bookmarks window.

FIGURE 8.2   The ESPNET SportsZone Home Page.

4. Select Edit Bookmarks to open the Bookmarks Properties dialog box (see Figure 8.3). Highlight ESPNET SportsZone. Open the Edit menu and choose Bookmark Properties to open the Bookmark Properties sheet (see Figure 8.4).

5. The title ESPNET SportsZone should be highlighted in the Name text box; if it's not, highlight it. Delete this title and enter ESPN Home Page. Click OK, and your bookmark list changes.

Most of the Web pages you include in your bookmark lists will not need to be edited. Occasionally, however, you will encounter Web pages for which the author has created an obscure title, a very long title, or no title at all. If a page does not have a title, the

URL becomes the title. In a case like that, you might want to edit the title of your bookmark to give it a more meaningful title.

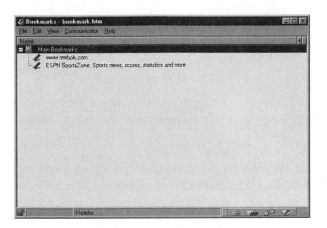

FIGURE 8.3   The Bookmark Properties dialog box.

FIGURE 8.4   The Bookmark Properties sheet.

DELETING BOOKMARKS

Periodically, Web pages change or move, or you just get tired of a particular page you've placed in your list of bookmarks and decide you want to cull your list of less desirable pages. To see how this

works, add a bookmark that you probably would not keep on
your list, and then delete it:

1. Jump to the following URL and add it to your list of book-
    marks, as you learned in the previous section.

    **http://wwwtios.cs.utwente.nl/~kenter/
    spam.html**

    This takes you to a Spam! Web page.

2. Click the Bookmark button on the Location toolbar and
    select Edit Bookmarks to open the Bookmarks dialog box.

3. Select Spam!.

4. Select Edit, Delete, (or press the Delete key) and Spam! is
    gone (thank goodness!).

ORGANIZING BOOKMARKS WITH MENUS

Creating and editing bookmarks is not all Netscape lets you do.
You can also create menu titles, or folders to group your menu
items together. To create a menu folder along with the two bookmarks you added earlier, follow these steps:

1. Open the Bookmarks menu and choose Edit Bookmarks
    to open the Bookmark Properties dialog box.

2. Select ESPNET SportsZone. Open the File menu and
    choose New Folder to open the Bookmark Properties
    sheet. Delete the contents of the Name text box, and
    enter **Sports**. Click OK. The new header Sports appears
    below **ESPN Home Page**.

3. Click ESPN Home Page, hold down the left mouse button,
    drag it down to the Sports header, and release the mouse
    button. The ESPN Home Page bookmark appears under
    the Sports header (see Figure 8.5).

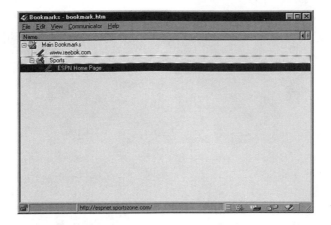

FIGURE 8.5 The ESPN Home Page bookmark is under the Sports menu folder.

4. Close the Netscape Bookmark properties dialog box. Select the Home icon to return to Netscape's Home Page. From the Netscape menu bar, choose Bookmarks. Notice that the bookmarks have changed. Choose Sports, and the menu folder appears displaying the ESPN Home Page bookmark. Choose the ESPN Home Page bookmark to jump to the ESPN home page (see Figure 8.6).

USING THE CUSTOMIZABLE TOOLBAR

One more cool trick you can do with Netscape's bookmarks is to place some of your most frequently used bookmarks close-at-hand. You can place these bookmarks on the Personal toolbar.

1. Click the Bookmarks button on the Location toolbar and select Edit Bookmarks to open the Bookmark properties dialog box.

2. Highlight the folder you created earlier, Sports.

3. Select File, Add Selection to Toolbar and a new folder is created called the Personal toolbar folder.

4. Close the Bookmark properties dialog box.

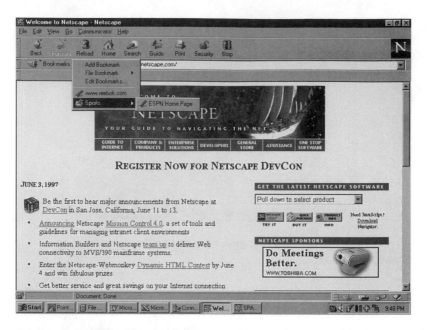

FIGURE 8.6 The Sports header submenu.

5. Look at the Personal toolbar and you'll notice that there is now a button on the toolbar named **Sports**; if you click the new Sports button, you'll see a copy of the Sports folder you created earlier in this lesson (see Figure 8.7).

You can add folders or bookmarks directly to your Personal toolbar and make them just a little bit closer for you to use.

In this lesson, you learned how to record Web pages you've visited by creating bookmarks in Netscape. In the next lesson, you learn how to configure Netscape to use plug-ins.

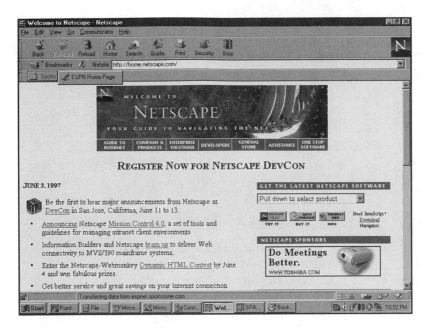

FIGURE 8.7 You can add the Sports folder on the Personal Toolbar.

USING NETSCAPE PLUG-INS

In this lesson, you learn about the application extensions for Netscape, called plug-ins.

WHAT ARE PLUG-INS?

In Netscape Navigator version 2.0, Netscape introduced a new feature for its popular Web browser. *Plug-ins* are extensions you add to the basic Netscape browser to expand its capabilities. When you run across certain files on the Web, such as audio or video files, plug-ins enable you to play the files without having to exit Navigator or open a new program. Many plug-ins work so well with Netscape that you don't even know they are not a basic part of the core Netscape application.

 Ever Heard of a Helper App? Helper apps are similar to plug-ins, but they aren't as closely integrated into Netscape Navigator. Helper apps are also more limited in the tasks they can perform.

When a plug-in is installed and activated, it can function in one of three ways:

- As an embedded application, which appears as a visible rectangular window created by a graphic (much like a GIF or JPEG picture).

- As a full-screen application, which takes over the entire Netscape window to operate.

- As a hidden application, which does not appear to change the appearance of Netscape, but merely serves to extend Netscape's functionality.

This lesson takes a look at a few of the more popular Netscape plug-ins, specifically the plug-ins that are pre-installed in the basic Netscape 4.0 package.

LiveAudio enables you to instantly hear audio files embedded in Web pages, without waiting for the entire file to download. It supports the following audio formats (among others): .WAV (Windows Waveform), .AU/.SND (Sun/NeXT Audio), .AIF/.AIFF (Mac audio), and .MID/MIDI (Midi Music).

QuickTime enables you to play real-time video files in the QuickTime™ format.

Cosmo is a virtual reality plug-in with which you can view and manipulate 3-D objects created using the Virtual Reality Modeling Language (VRML). These objects are often found on Web pages.

Because Netscape is distributed as a multiplatform application, the plug-in features described in this lesson may not appear in all versions of Netscape, especially the 16-bit Windows version and some versions of UNIX.

LiveAudio

Live or real-time audio has been present on the Internet in some form for more than two years. Presently, there are about a half dozen competing audio programs, most of which have their own audio file format. This has created a glaring problem: none of the programs can play the audio files of the competing programs. Netscape's LiveAudio plug-in seems to solve this problem. LiveAudio plays, almost instantly, most of the common, popular audio formats in use today. If you double-click an audio file that you encounter on the Web, Netscape automatically starts LiveAudio, which plays the sound file.

Instead of talking about LiveAudio, let's have a demonstration. If you don't already have Netscape started, start the program and use the following URL to jump to the Beatles Jukebox Web site: **http://www.geocities.com/Yosemite/2729/**. When you first display this site one of the audio files begins playing automatically (see Figure 9.1).

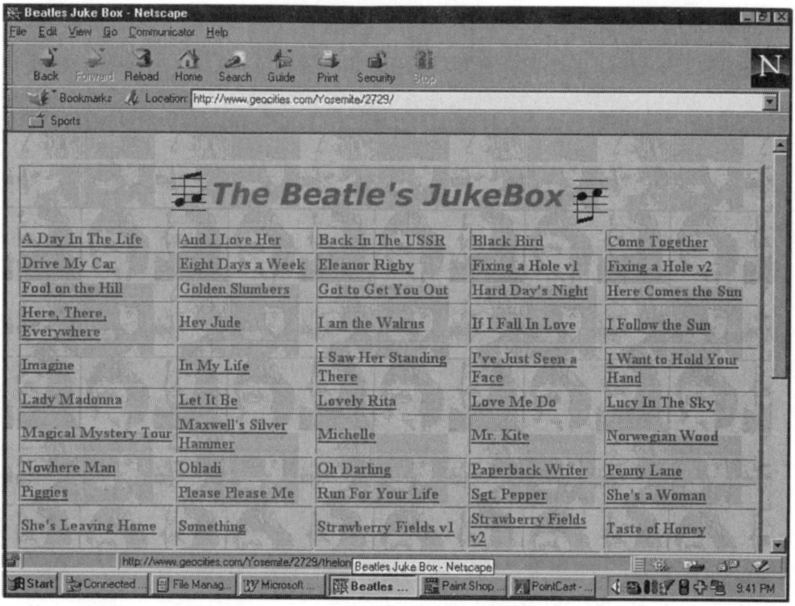

FIGURE 9.1   The Beatles Jukebox Web site.

> **I Don't Hear Anything!**   You must have a sound card installed in your PC to hear the files played by LiveAudio. You cannot use one of the "PC speaker drivers" available on many FTP sites.

Make sure your sound card is installed and your speakers are turned on, because when you first arrive at the Beatles Jukebox Web site, you're greeted by Lovely Rita (from the Sgt. Pepper album), which is the first LiveAudio demonstration. Spend as much time as you like and listen to as many tunes as you like. If your music tastes run to a slightly different genre, then try either the Led Zeppelin Jukebox site or the Pop/Rock Jukebox site. Both have links at the bottom of the page.

> **Streaming Audio**   Did you notice that even though most of the songs on the Beatles Jukebox site averaged 3 to 4 minutes in length, it only took a few seconds for the tunes to begin? You didn't have to wait for the entire song to download before it began playing. What you experienced was an example of *streaming audio.* Streaming audio is a technique which allows Netscape to play audio files as they are being downloaded to your computer and not force you to wait for the entire file to be downloaded before you can listen to it.

QUICKTIME

QuickTime is a real-time movie format developed by Apple Computer Company and is one of the dominant real-time movie formats on the Internet.

Again, rather than tell you about QuickTime movies, let me take you to a site where you can sample QuickTime movies for yourself.

Jump to **http://film.softcenter.se/flics/**, The QuickTime Archive (see Figure 9.2).

To select a movie trailer at this site, select the letter which begins the name of the movie trailer you want to view. For example, to select a trailer for Independence Day select I and then follow the prompts to select one of the available QuickTime movies (see Figure 9.3).

If you're interested in viewing more QuickTime movies or finding out more about the QuickTime format, here is a list of a few sites you might want to visit:

- Video Links **http://members.aol.com/videolinks/ index.html**

- Modern Television **http://www.moderntv.com/ modtvweb/viewrec/videoqt1.htm**

- QuickTime Home Page **http:// www.quicktime.apple.com/**

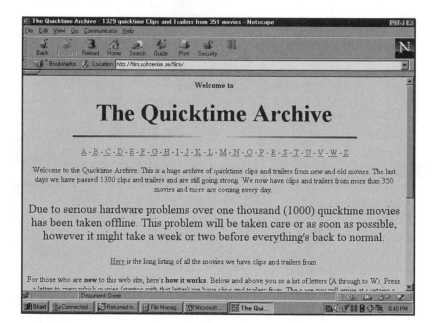

FIGURE 9.2   The QuickTime Archive.

COSMO

Cosmo is a VRML (Virtual Reality Modeling Language) plug-in which is included with Netscape Communicator. VRML is a way of creating virtual reality sites which you can move through much the same as you would move through actual 3-D objects.

To try Cosmo, let's go to the Cosmo Web site gallery at **http:// vrml.sgi.com/worlds/** (see Figure 9.4).

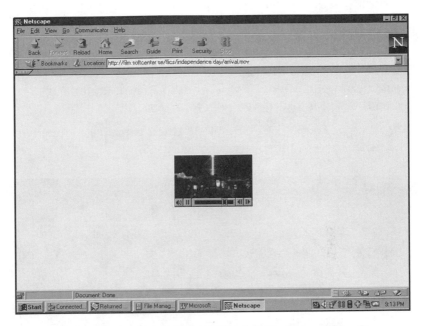

FIGURE 9.3   QuickTime movie trailer from Independence Day.

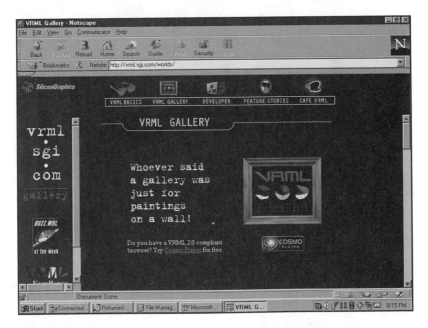

FIGURE 9.4   The Cosmo Web site VRML Gallery.

There are several dozen VRML pages you can explore here. To enter a VRML page, select the link and then wait for the VRML page to download and display. Depending on the speed of your Internet connection and the speed of your computer, the wait could be anywhere from a few seconds to a few minutes. But when the page is loaded, you're in for a treat.

For example, take a look at the VRML Chess game page located on the second page of the gallery (see Figure 9.5).

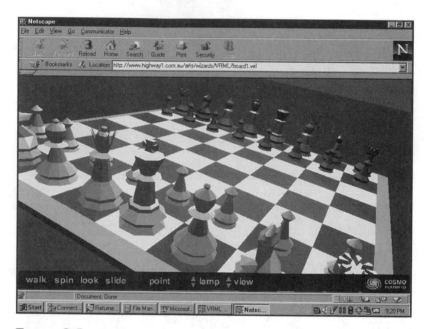

FIGURE 9.5   A VRML chess game on the Cosmo Web site.

ACQUIRING MORE PLUG-INS

You can acquire as many plug-ins as you need, and one of the best places to locate plug-ins and inquire about new plug-ins is at Netscape's own plug-in page at **http://home.netscape.com/ comprod/products/navigator/version_2.0/plugins/ index.html** (see Figure 9.6).

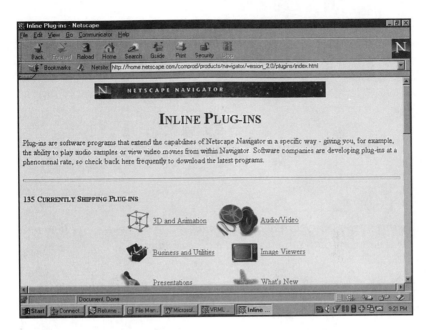

FIGURE 9.6   Netscape's Plug-in page.

> 💡 **What Plug-Ins do I Have Loaded?**   Anytime you want to check to see which plug-ins are installed with your copy of Netscape, select Help, About Plug-ins in Netscape to display the list of plug-ins you've installed.

In this lesson, you learned how to use Netscape plug-ins, specifically, the plug-ins shipped with Netscape Communicator. In the next lesson, you will learn how to install plug-ins by installing the RealPlayer plug-in, the successor to one of the most popular Netscape plug-ins, RealAudio.

REAL-TIME AUDIO AND VIDEO USING THE REALPLAYER

In this lesson, you learn about streaming audio and video and how to configure your browser to use the RealPlayer plug-in.

PLAYING AUDIO AND VIDEO WITH THE REALPLAYER

In the last lesson you learned about plug-ins and how they can be used to extend the capability of Netscape Navigator. Now it's time to learn just how easy it is to install a Netscape plug-in. Actually you will be installing two plug-ins—RealAudio and RealPlayer.

REALAUDIO

RealAudio is one of the most amazing and interesting sound re-production systems available on the Internet. It seems to solve one of the major problems in delivering multimedia sound over the Internet for users who use a Web browser other than Netscape. With RealAudio, there is virtually no limit to the length of audio files you can hear over the Internet. In fact, the RealAudio system is used to transmit live audio broadcast over the Internet.

RealAudio compresses the audio stream as it's sent down the Internet to your computer and buffers the stream as it's received. This means that you hear the sound a few seconds after your computer receives it. The technique LiveAudio uses is based on the

RealAudio audio stream principle. One difference you may notice between RealAudio and LiveAudio is that RealAudio, being a more mature product, produces a higher quality sound. Over the years since it was initially released, RealAudio has been gradually improving the quality of sound it can deliver over the Internet. Now with a good quality soundcard and speakers, RealAudio is very near CD-quality sound.

RealAudio is available for all flavors of Windows, the Mac, and several UNIX platforms. To install RealAudio on your PC, follow these steps:

1. Use your Web browser to jump to the RealAudio Home Page (see Figure 10.1), located at **http://www. realaudio.com/**.

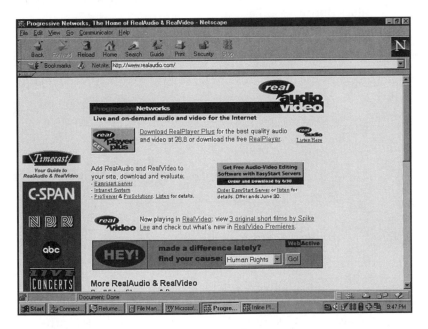

FIGURE 10.1   The RealAudio Home Page.

2. Select the RealAudio Player links, and follow the prompts to download the RealAudio Player for your operating system platform.

> 💡 **Print the FAQs**   It's helpful to print the RealAudio FAQ
> page and the RealAudio Player FAQ page. Both pages
> contain valuable information on configuring and trouble-
> shooting RealAudio. To get to the RealAudio FAQ page,
> click the RealAudio Player FAQ link on the RealAudio
> Player Download Page. Click the Configure Your Web
> Browser link to get to the RealAudio Player FAQ page.

3. The file you downloaded is in a compressed archive format, so you will have to decompress the file before you
   can install it. To decompress the archive, run the file the
   same as you would any program or application. Follow
   the prompts to install RealAudio, accepting the default
   values during installation.

4. When the installation is complete, restart your Web
   browser and go back to the RealAudio Home Page.

> 💡 **Create Bookmarks**   You'll certainly save yourself a few
> headaches later if you create bookmarks as you go
> through each lesson. To return to Web pages you like, it's
> a lot easier to open the Bookmarks menu and choose
> Add Bookmark (or press Ctrl+A) than it is to go back
> through each lesson and try to locate each URL.

5. Scroll down to the Site Map link at the bottom of the
   page, or use the Sites and Sounds image map to the left of
   the page to see some of the organizations currently using
   RealAudio.

6. Click the ABC logo to jump to the ABC page, select one of
   the available links, and then listen. In a few seconds, the
   RealAudio Player appears, as you see in Figure 10.2. A few
   seconds later, you should hear an audio report that lasts a
   few minutes.

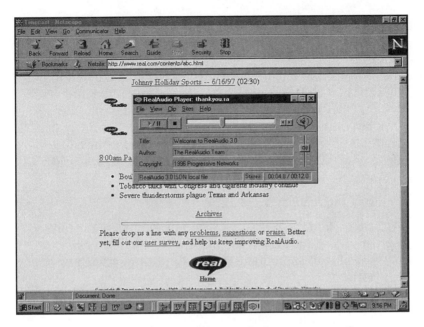

FIGURE 10.2 The RealAudio Player window appears when you play an audio file.

![alarm clock icon] **I Don't Hear Anything!** It's possible (for a variety of reasons too numerous to list here) that RealAudio doesn't work on your system. Go back and take a look at the two FAQ pages mentioned earlier to see if either page sheds any light on your audio problem. Also, double-check your installation procedure to make sure that you didn't skip any steps. Finally, open the Options menu and choose Preferences. From the Set Preferences On drop-down list, select Helper Applications. Check to make sure there is a reference to the RealAudio player and that Netscape is looking into the folder where the RealAudio player is installed. If everything checks out okay, you might want to check with your service provider to make sure RealAudio is not being blocked by your provider.

THE REALPLAYER AS A NETSCAPE PLUG-IN

The developers at Progressive Networks were not content to produce the best and most popular audio system on the Internet. Recently they released the successor to RealAudio—RealPlayer. RealPlayer is both an audio and video playback system, and like RealAudio, RealPlayer does not make you wait for the entire video file to download before you can view it (as you experienced back in Lesson 8 with QuickTime movies).

To install the RealPlayer plug-in:

1. Go back to the RealAudio Web site and follow the links to download the RealPlayer plug-in. Make sure you select the plug-in appropriate to your operating system platform.

2. Decompress and install the RealPlayer archive file just as you did with the RealAudio file.

3. Restart Netscape, just as before, and jump to the RealPlayer Customizing page (see Figure 10.3).

4. On the Customizing page you can preset your RealPlayer to specific Web sites which regularly broadcast audio and video feeds for the RealPlayer.

After you browse some of the sites and pages where RealPlayer can be used, you might notice that some pages require you to register for a free user account. RealPlayer and RealVideo site developers probably use this method to track the number of people on the Internet who use and view RealVideo. If you plan to use the RealPlayer in the future, go ahead and register.

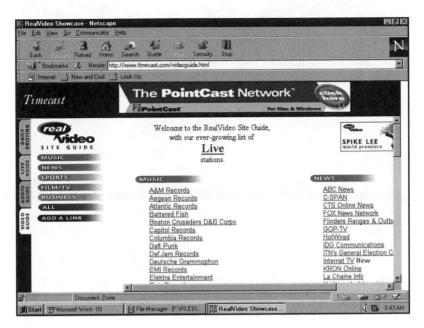

FIGURE. 10.3   The RealPlayer Customizing page.

In this lesson, you learned about playing audio and video files on the Web with Netscape, RealAudio, and RealPlayer. In the next lesson, you learn about offline Web browsing and how to subscribe to Web sites.

SEARCHING THE INTERNET USING SEARCH ENGINES

In this lesson, you learn how to search for Web pages using some of the Internet's best search engines: Yahoo, Lycos, AltaVista, and HotBot.

WHAT IS A SEARCH ENGINE?

So far, all of the Web pages you've seen in this book have been pages you've been directed to in various lessons. However, you don't have to wait around for someone to tell you about Web pages and where to find them. You can locate them yourself by using a search engine. A *search engine* (on the World Wide Web) is a program that analyzes Web page titles and keeps track of the information they contain. It allows you to enter a search request, called a query, and then gives you a list of Web pages that matches your query. Two of the most popular search engines on the Web are Yahoo and Lycos.

SEARCHING WITH YAHOO

Yahoo, which was started a few years ago at Stanford University by two graduate students, now ranks as one of the most popular Web search engines. Netscape contains a built-in link to Yahoo so you can get there quickly.

To get to Yahoo in Netscape, follow these steps:

1. Click the Search toolbar button. This takes you to Netscape's Search page.

> **I Don't Have Any Directory Buttons!**   If Netscape's toolbar buttons don't appear across your screen, you may have hidden them. Open the View menu and select the Show Navigation Toolbar menu option. If you don't want to turn toolbar buttons on, you can go directly to Yahoo by typing **http://www.yahoo.com** in the Open Page dialog box and pressing Enter. You might even want to create a bookmark for it.

2. Click the Yahoo link (see Figure 11.1) to go to the Yahoo search engine.

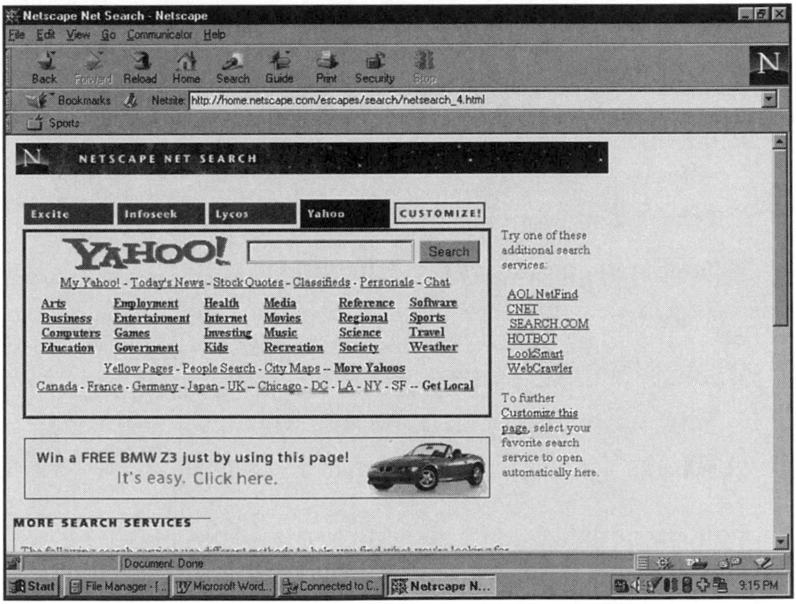

FIGURE 11.1   The Yahoo link on Netscape's Search page.

To get to Yahoo using Internet Explorer, enter **http://www.yahoo.com/** in the Address text box. This takes you directly to Yahoo. (There is no Yahoo link on the Internet Explorer Home Page.)

My Netscape Net Search Page Looks Different! Don't panic if your Search page is different from the one shown in Figure 11.1. Netscape (like many other Web sites) changes its appearance every few months.

You can search in Yahoo using either of two methods. You can search a categorized list of Web pages organized under 14 major categories, or you can enter a search query. Those methods are covered in detail in the following sections.

SEARCHING BY CATEGORY

Because Yahoo already has a long list of Web pages organized by category, you can search Yahoo by stepping through links along the established categories and subcategories. Here are the Yahoo categories:

Arts	News and Media
Business and Economy	Recreation and Sports
Computers and Internet	Reference
Education	Regional
Entertainment	Science
Government	Social Science
Health	Society and Culture

Suppose, for example, you wanted to locate Web pages that contain information on the Grand Canyon. Here's how you would use Yahoo:

1. At the Yahoo Home Page, click the Regional link. Clicking this link takes you to Yahoo's Regional page.

2. At the Regional page, click the U.S. States link to go to the Regional:U.S. States page.

3. At the Regional:U.S. States page, click the Arizona link to go to the Regional:U.S. States:Arizona page.

4. At the Regional:U.S. States:Arizona page, click the Grand Canyon link to go to the Regional:U.S. States:Arizona:Grand Canyon page, which is the object of your search (see Figure 11.2).

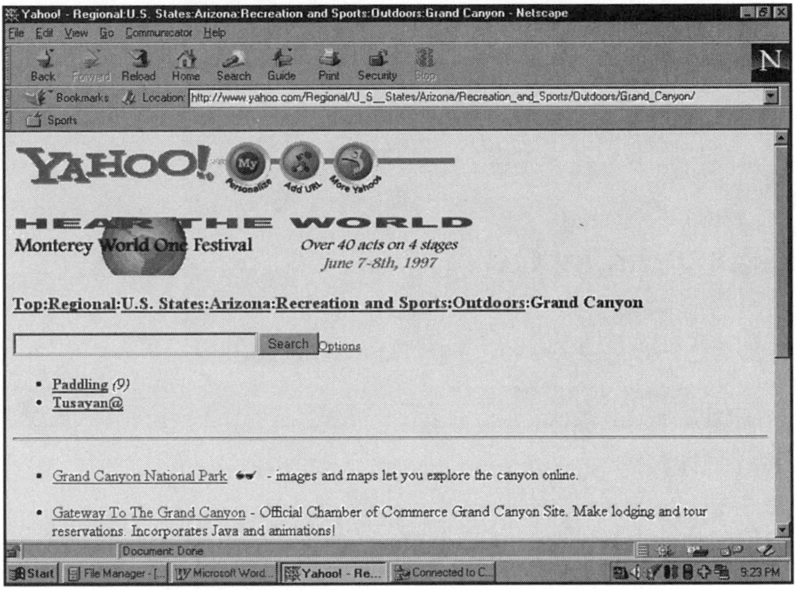

FIGURE 11.2   The Regional:U.S. States:Arizona:Grand Canyon page.

At this point, you're free to examine any or all of the Grand Canyon links. If you have a few minutes, click the Grand Canyon Tour link to go the page shown in Figure 11.3. Besides receiving a wealth of interesting facts about the world's most popular canyon, you'll find links to breathtaking photos.

FINDING A TOPIC BY KEYWORD

Most of the major search engines conduct searches by keyword, which by the way, Yahoo is also capable of doing. For this example though, let's take a look at a keyword search using AltaVista.

FIGURE 11.3   Scenes from the Grand Canyon tour.

AltaVista allows you to conduct a search by typing a word or phrase as your query. To do so, follow these steps:

1. Go to the AltaVista Home Page at **http://www. altavista.digital.com** (see Figure 11.4), and enter a keyword in the query field. For this example, enter the keyword eclipses to find pages with information pertaining to solar or lunar eclipses.

2. Click the Submit button. The results of your query will appear in a few seconds (see Figure 11.5).

3. From the results page, you can click any link to go to a matching page that interests you. When you reach the bottom of this page, select the next number in the display to advance to the next results page.

Most of time you will likely be conducting single word searches, usually on a specific category or idea. But AltaVista also allows you to modify your search parameters using its advanced search options. Using it's search syntax, you can combine words to either expand or narrow your search. For example, suppose I want to search for eclipses again, but I only want solar eclipses and not lunar eclipses. I could conduct a search using **eclipses AND NOT lunar** and my search would only give me a list of pages pertaining to solar eclipses.

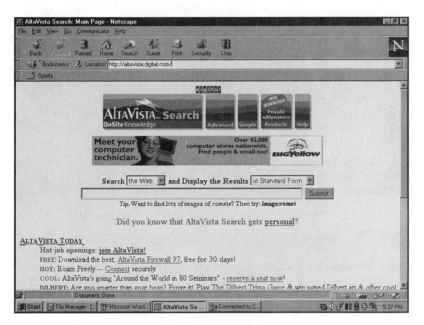

FIGURE 11.4   The AltaVista Home Page.

To find out more about conducting advanced searches in AltaVista, click the Advanced link located on AltaVista's masthead.

LYCOS

Another popular Internet search engine is Lycos, which was started by Carnegie Mellon University in Pittsburgh, but is now a separate, independent entity. You can find Lycos at **http://www.lycos.com/**.

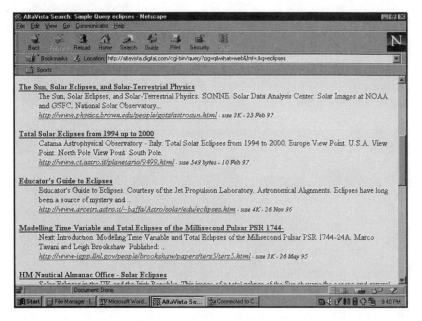

FIGURE 11.5   Results of AltaVista's search for the word "eclipses."

Lycos is a very large database, which recently added a host of new Internet feature services to its original query capabilities.

Figure 11.6 shows the standard database search engine. It works like the keyword search engine in AltaVista, and it has most of the same options as AltaVista for modifying your query parameters.

HOTBOT

Another search engine which seems to be stealing a lot of the thunder from AltaVista and Lycos is HotBot, located at **http://www.hotbot.com** (see Figure 11.7).

For many, HotBot may be a bit easier to use than either AltaVista or Lycos, because you do not have to concern yourself with using the proper syntax in a query containing multiple keywords. While you can use keyword search syntax similar to what you would use in AltaVista, HotBot gives you a simple drop-down menu, which should handle approximately 70–80 percent of your search queries.

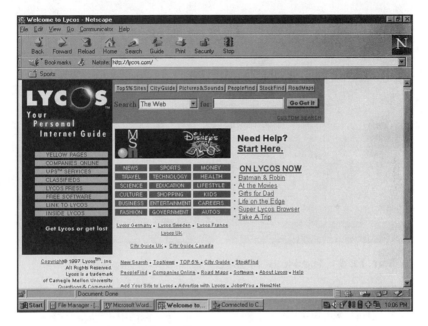

FIGURE 11.6   Lycos Home Page.

If you're wondering which search engine to use, you're not alone. Take these things into consideration:

- If you're searching on a topic that you think is more mainstream, try Yahoo first. The editors at Yahoo do not even try to include each and every Web page in existence. They tend to be somewhat selective when deciding what to include in their database. Yahoo is, therefore, a lot smaller and a lot faster than Lycos, AltaVista, or most of the other search engines.

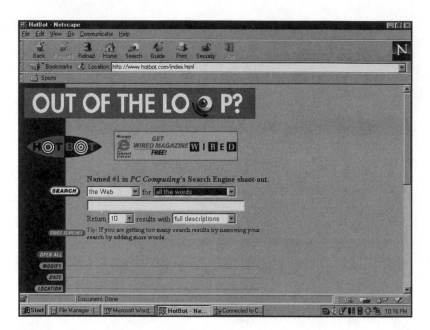

FIGURE 11.7   The HotBot Home Page.

- If, on the other hand, your search parameters are somewhat obscure, or if the topic is not necessarily something
  that pops up in everyday conversation, Lycos or HotBot
  will generally produce better results because its database is
  more than 10 times larger than Yahoo's. If you are conducting complex searches AltaVista may be your best bet.

OTHER SEARCH ENGINES

If Yahoo, Lycos, AltaVista, or HotBot don't meet your needs, try
one of the search engines listed here.

- WebCrawler at **http://www.webcrawler.com**

  WebCrawler is another robot search engine. Like Lycos, it
  uses a search technique that actually visits other Internet
  sites to gather information about its database. This technique produces a fairly large, fairly comprehensive database of Internet sites, pages, and information.

- Infoseek at **http://www2.infoseek.com**

  Infoseek is a commercial search engine that boasts a very large following, or at least a very busy search engine (one million search requests per day). It's geared more toward commercial users (large commercial database; quick turn-around).

- New Riders' Official WWW Yellow Pages at **http:// www.mcp.com/nrp/wwwyp**

  This is the online version of the NRP WWW Yellow Pages. It is, by design, a tool used only to search the World Wide Web and has a very extensive and diverse Web database.

- Magellan at **http://www.mckinley.com/**

  Magellan is a service that bills itself as an Internet Guide, as opposed to a search engine. Its database is categorized into 27 contemporary topics. Magellan is good on current events, news, and popular sites.

In this lesson, you learned how to use some of the most popular search engines used on the World Wide Web. In the next lesson, you learn about sending and receiving e-mail.

12 SENDING AND RECEIVING E-MAIL

In this lesson, you learn how to use Microsoft's Outlook Express to send and receive e-mail over the Internet.

CONFIGURING OUTLOOK EXPRESS

If you previously installed Microsoft's Internet Explorer 4.0, you have already installed an Internet e-mail client. Besides offering a great Web browser, IE4 also includes a full-featured e-mail program in the same package. Outlook Express includes a hierarchical filing system, HTML coding in messages, ability to handle multiple e-mail accounts, and can double as a newsreader.

All you need to do to use Outlook Express is set a few configuration parameters:

1. Start Outlook Express. In Windows 95 and NT 4.0 the Outlook Express icon is just to the right of the Start menu. Open the Tools menu and select Mail Options to open the Mail Options dialog box (see Figure 12.1).

2. In the Send sheet, under the Mail Sending settings, select all of the options listed. Saving a copy of each message sent in the Sent Mail folder gives you a copy of your outgoing messages. Including the text of the original message in your replies makes it easier for people to remember what their original message contained. Sending messages immediately means your messages are sent as soon as you press the Send button and do not clutter your Outbox. And setting Outlook Express as your default e-mail program is merely a preference.

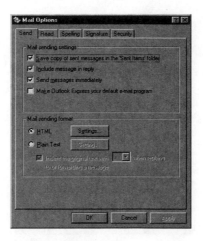

FIGURE 12.1   The Mail Options dialog box.

3. In the Mail sending format section select Plain Text unless you are sure everyone you will be corresponding with uses an HTML capable e-mail client (IE4 Outlook Express and Netscape Messenger are, but most other e-mail clients are not).

4. Use the last controls in this section to indicate how you want Outlook Express to handle mail messages after you have read them, and how often you want Outlook Express to check your mail server for new e-mail messages. If you want the original text of messages you are replying to, to be indented with an indent character, select the check box below the plain text formatter and select a character to use.

5. Click the Read tab to display the setting used for reading your incoming e-mail messages (see Figure 12.2).

6. If you want Outlook Express to notify you with a sound when you have new mail select the check box Play Sound When New Message Arrives.

7. The option Mark Message as Read After Previewed for [0–60] Seconds is merely a convenience. Selection is optional.

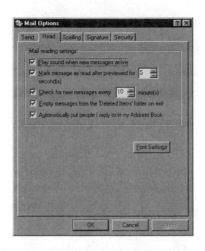

FIGURE 12.2   The Read sheet in the Mail Options dialog box.

8. If you want Outlook Express to periodically check your mailbox for new message select the Check for New Messages Every [1–120] Minutes check box.

9. I would recommend you select the Empty Messages from the 'Deleted Items' Folder on Exit check box to help reduce clutter on your hard disk.

10. I would also recommend you select the Automatically Put People I Reply to in my Address Book check box, again as a convenience to you.

11. You can change the font selection in Font Settings (see Figure 12.3) if you like. This is just a matter of preference.

12. Click the Spelling tab to display the setting used to have Outlook Express check the spelling of the messages you create (see Figure 12.4).

13. All of the spelling settings are a matter of preference, so decide which if any you want to set or change.

14. If you want to add words to your custom dictionary, select the Edit Custom Dictionary button.

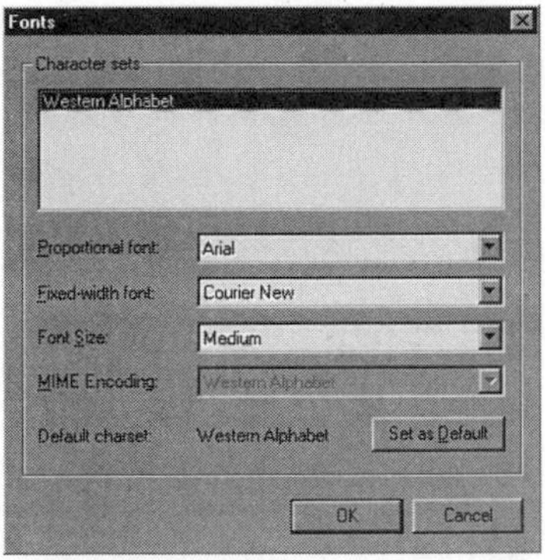

FIGURE 12.3   The Font Settings of the Read sheet in the Mail Options dialog box.

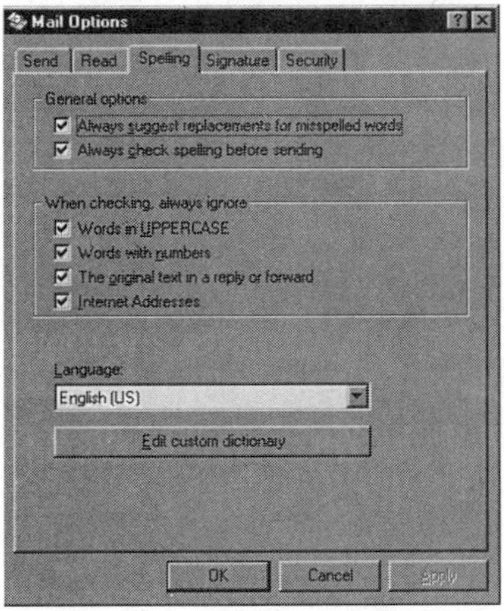

FIGURE 12.4   The Spelling sheet in the Mail Options dialog box.

15. Click the Signature tab to display the setting used to have Outlook Express add a signature to the messages you create (see Figure 12.5).

> **Signature**   A tag placed at the end of your e-mail messages. The tag can be a witty or humorous saying, or something profound you want to share with those you communicate with.

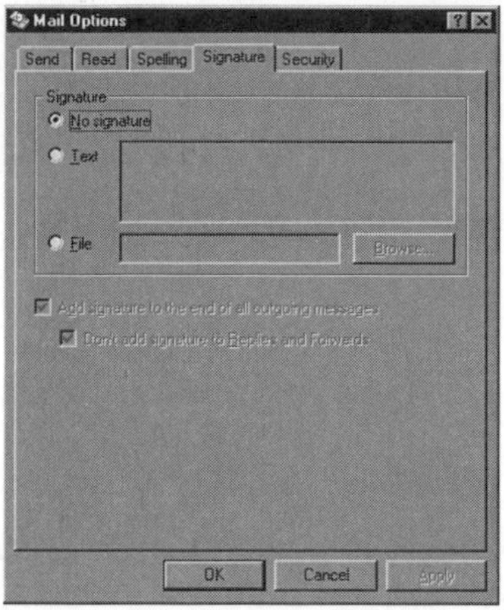

FIGURE 12.5   The Signature sheet in the Mail Options dialog box.

16. Click the Security tab to display the setting used to make your e-mail messages secure (see Figure 12.6).

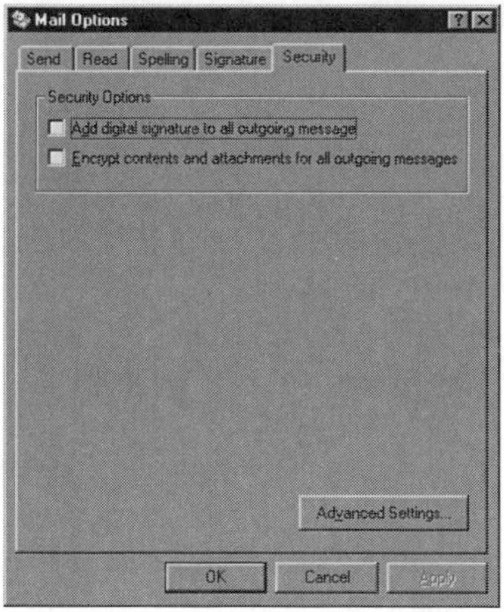

FIGURE 12.6   The Security sheet in the Mail Options dialog box.

17. Click OK to save your configuration settings.

> **Do I Really Need to be Concerned about Securing my E-mail Messages?**   If you regularly send sensitive or confidential information, you might want to consider encrypting your e-mail messages. Outlook Express is capable of sending encrypted messages, but to do so you will need to obtain a digital ID. To get your digital ID and to find out more about encryption and e-mail security, take a look at the Verisign Web site at **http://www. verisign.com/**.

KEEPING TRACK OF PEOPLE WITH YOUR ADDRESS BOOK

Before you start sending mail, you should take care of one small housekeeping chore: setting up your Address Book. The Address Book contains the names and e-mail addresses of people to whom you regularly send e-mail. You can also use the address book to create groups of people you regularly communicate with in mailing lists.

> **Address Books Save Time**   You'll save some time if you enter the names and e-mail addresses of people you send mail to often. If these names and addresses are not in your Address Book, you have to manually type the names and addresses each time you want to send e-mail.

To enter names into your personal Address Book:

1. Select Tools, Address Book to open the Address Book window. You can also press Ctrl+Shift+B, or select the Address Book button on the toolbar.

2. To enter a name in your address book, select File, New Contact or select the New Contact toolbar button to open the New Contact Properties dialog box (see Figure 12.7).

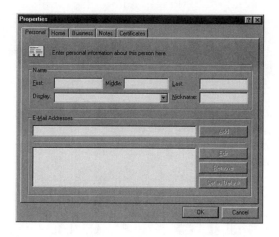

FIGURE 12.7   The New Contact properties dialog box.

3. Enter the first, middle, and last name of the person you are entering along with their e-mail address. All other fields are optional. If you like, you can also select the Home, Business, and Notes tabs to enter additional information about this person. If this person has a digital ID, they can send you a copy of their public key which will appear in your certificates listing for this person. Select Add to add this entry to your Address Book.

> **What Do I Add**   If you are at loss for someone's name to enter, you can enter mine. My e-mail address is gagrimes@city-net.com. I won't promise I will be able to answer everyone who sends me a message, but I will try.

4. Click OK to save the entry in your Address Book and close the dialog box. You can also close the Address Book by selecting File, Close.

CREATING AND SENDING E-MAIL

The main purpose of any e-mail application is to send e-mail, so jump right in and send your first e-mail message.

1. Open the File menu and select New, Message, or click the New Message icon on the toolbar. The Outlook Express New Message dialog box opens, in which you compose your e-mail message (see Figure 12.8).

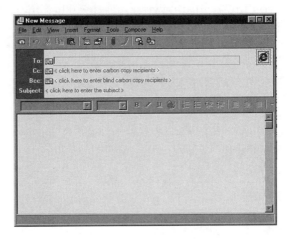

FIGURE **12.8** The New Message dialog box.

2. Type the e-mail address of the person to whom you are sending the message in the To: field. Or, if the person's address is in your Address Book, select the Address icon to open your Address Book. In the Address Book, select the person's name, click To:, and click OK.

3. (Optional) If you want to send a carbon copy (CC) of this message to someone, type his e-mail address in the Cc: field. Or, open the Address Book, select the person's name, click Cc:, and click OK. Repeat this procedure and select BCC to send a blind carbon copy.

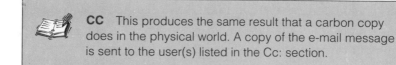

CC This produces the same result that a carbon copy does in the physical world. A copy of the e-mail message is sent to the user(s) listed in the Cc: section.

4. (Optional) Enter a subject in the Subject: field.

5. Click in the message window and type your message.

6. When you finish creating your message, click the Send icon (the first toolbar icon, the one that looks like an envelope) to send the message.

What Does Each Icon Do? To learn what each icon does, you can check the Help system. Or you can simply place your cursor on each icon, and in 1–2 seconds, a label appears describing the function of that particular icon.

RECEIVING E-MAIL

After you start sending e-mail, it won't be long before someone responds to one of your messages. To check to see if you have messages waiting, follow these steps:

1. Open the Tools menu and choose Receive, All Accounts, or click the Send and Receive icon to check your mail server for new mail messages. If you have any messages waiting, they will be retrieved from your mail server and they will appear in your Inbox (see Figure 12.9).

2. To read a message in your Inbox, select the message you want to read and the message will appear in the lower half of the Inbox.

FIGURE 12.9   Receiving new e-mail messages.

OTHER INTERNET E-MAIL PROGRAMS

Outlook Express is a good and easy choice for people using IE4. You can, however, choose different Internet e-mail programs if you want.

Netscape messenger is part of the Netscape Communicator suite and works quite well as an Internet mail client. Three other popular e-mail programs you can try are Pegasus, E-mail Connection, and Eudora:

- You can download Pegasus from the mail section of the C/Net Web site at **http://www.download.com**.

- You can download E-mail Connection from **http://www.connectsoft.com/**.

- You can find the shareware version of Eudora on most FTP sites.

Each program comes with a complete set of instructions and help files. Using what you have learned in this lesson, you should have no trouble installing and running any of them.

In this lesson, you learned how to use Netscape e-mail as your Internet e-mail program. In the next lesson, you learn about accessing FTP servers using a graphical FTP utility.

ACCESSING FILES WITH FTP

In this lesson, you learn how to use two different FTP programs to download files.

WHAT IS THE WINDOWS 95 FTP?

Windows 95 includes a few Internet utilities, one of which is FTP. FTP, short for File Transfer Protocol, is a very useful program that allows you to transfer all types of files from an Internet computer, called an FTP server, to your PC. The only problem, which you will see firsthand, is that the FTP utility included with Windows 95 is a text-based console program that's a bit cumbersome to use. Fortunately, you will only need to use it in this lesson. Afterward, you will never have to use it again because, in this lesson, you will use it to download a Windows-based FTP utility that's a lot easier to use.

UNIX users already have an FTP program—a standard UNIX utility. Users running Windows 3.1 or Mac can easily secure an FTP utility from their Internet service provider, which should also provide instructions for using it.

> **Download**   An old mainframe computer term that simply means to copy a file or program from a host computer "down" to your computer. And as you might have guessed, the opposite of download is upload, which means to copy a file from your computer "up" to the host computer.

Virus Alert! Be aware that when you access an FTP server, you are potentially exposing your computer to computer viruses. Most server administrators scan all files that come into their servers, but occasionally some infected files do get in. Always make sure you run an up-to-date antivirus program before you download files. Also, make sure the antivirus programs (some experts recommend using more than one) you use are specifically made for your operating system. The best antivirus programs also can be configured in an "auto-protect" mode, meaning the program is constantly running and monitoring your system for viruses and virus-like activity (such as formatting, changing file attributes, and so on).

USING **FTP**

To use the Windows 95 FTP utility, first make sure that you connect to your Internet provider. Then follow these steps:

1. Select the Start button on the taskbar and choose Run .

2. In the Run dialog box type **ftp** and press Enter. FTP starts, and you see the FTP prompt.

3. For this lesson, you're going to log in to the FTP server gatekeeper.dec.com and download the file ws_ftp32.zip. To log in to gatekeeper.dec.com, type the command **open gatekeeper.dec.com**. (To log in to a different server, you would substitute its name for gatekeeper.dec.com.)

4. The FTP server will respond with the prompt User (gatekeeper.dec.com:(none)):. To log in, type the user name **anonymous**. Then you're prompted to enter a password. Enter your e-mail address as your password, and the FTP server grants you access.

5. The file you want is in the /pub/micro/pc/win3/winsock directory. To change to that directory, issue the change directory command cd directory, where directory is the

full directory path. For this example, type **cd pub/ micro/pc/win3/winsock**.

> **Got a File Compression Program?** Many files you find on FTP servers will be in a compressed archive format. To decompress files of this type, you need a compression/ decompression utility. For DOS/Windows files, you can get WinZip or PKUNZIP; for the Mac, look for a program called Stuffit; and UNIX users should pick up a copy of GZIP. If you don't have a compression/decompression program, you can download all three at gatekeeper.dec. com. The directories change sometimes, but you should be able to locate them under their respective platforms.

6. To download program files, enter the **binary** command before you begin the file download. This instructs the FTP server to prepare to do a binary (non-text) file download.

> **I Can't Log In!** FTP servers often have limits on the number of users who can log in at one time. When that limit is reached—which often happens on very popular servers—it will not permit any additional logins. If you get an error message to this effect, don't worry. Just try again later.

7. Enter the command **get filename drive:\newfilename** to download (get) the file you want (filename) to the drive with the file name you designate (newfilename). For this example, type **get ws_ftp32.zip c:\ws_ftp32.zip** and press Enter (see Figure 13.1). The file ws_ftp32.zip begins downloading to your C:\ drive. When the file is done downloading, the FTP server will indicate that the download is finished, how long it took, and the speed of the download.

8. To log out of the FTP server, type **quit** and press Enter. The ftp window closes.

Installing WS_FTP32

The file you downloaded, **ws_ftp32.zip**, is in a compressed archive format, so you need a program such as PKUNZIP to decompress it (I hope you also took the time to download that). To decompress **ws_ftp32.zip**, copy both files (pkunzip.exe and ws_ftp32.zip) into a folder, open a DOS window, type **pkunzip ws_ftp32**, and press Enter.

When ws_ftp32.zip finishes decompressing, install it as you would any other application in Windows 95. If you're not sure how to install an application in Windows 95, consult your Windows 95 documentation or Help system.

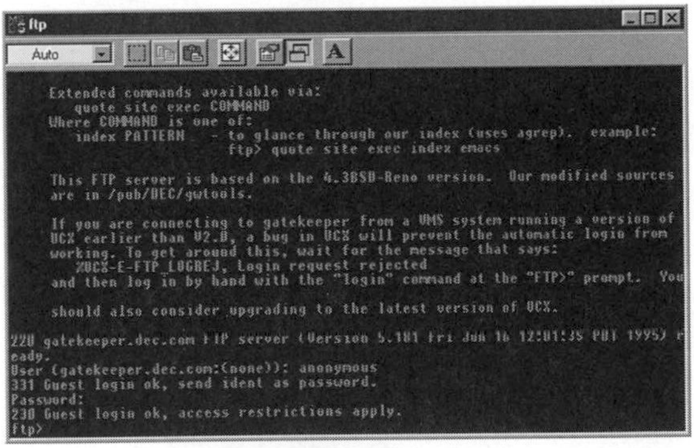

Figure 13.1   Download ws_ftp32.zip.

Running WS_FTP32/95

Now that you've installed WS_FTP32LE (or WS_FTP95LE), you're ready to start using WS_FTP32 as your FTP utility:

1. Click the Start button on the taskbar and choose Program, WS_FTP32 (which was created when you installed it). Now you can use WS_FTP32 to download some additional files that you will use in some of the later lessons. The Session Profile dialog box should appear.

2. If the Session Profile dialog box doesn't appear automatically, click the Connect button. In the Session Profile window, select the New button, and the Session Profile dialog box clears, ready for you to enter a new profile. You should probably take this opportunity to enter the profile information for the FTP site you just accessed—Gatekeeper (see Figure 13.2).

3. In the Profile Name drop-down list, select Gatekeeper. In the Host Name field, enter **gatekeeper.dec.com**. In the User ID field, enter **Anonymous** (or check the Anonymous Login check box). In the Password field, enter your full e-mail address (in my case, I would enter **gagrimes@city-net.com**). Select the Save Password check box. To save the information you entered, click the Save button.

4. Click OK to log in to Gatekeeper.

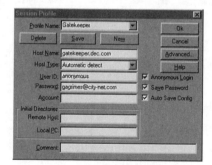

Figure 13.2   The Session Profile window of WS_FTP32.

💡 **Type Your Address Once**   If you select the Options button from the toolbar at the bottom of the screen, the Options dialog box appears. You can then select the Program Options button. You only have to enter your e-mail address once. Then, you simply have to select the Anonymous Login check box to enter your password. Just close the Session Profile dialog box first.

WS_FTP32's main screen is divided into two parts:

- The left side, identified as the Local System, shows the folders (directories) and files on your computer.

- The right side, identified as the Remote System, shows the folders (directories) and files on the computer you've logged in to.

Notice that each side is divided into an upper and lower portion or window. The upper portion shows the folders (directories) available to you on that drive or FTP server. The lower portion shows the files stored in the folder you are accessing. When more folders or files exist than fit in each portion, a scroll bar appears. Use it to navigate the list.

> **I Couldn't Log In!**   FTP servers often have limits regarding the number of users who can log in at one time. When that limit is reached—which often happens on very popular servers—it will not permit any additional logins. If you get an error message saying your login attempt failed, don't panic. Just try again later.

There are two arrows in the bar separating the Local System window from the Remote System window. One arrow points to the left and one arrow points to the right. Use these arrows to move files between the Remote and Local systems. To move a file from the Remote System to the Local System, highlight the file, and then click the arrow pointing to the left. To move a file from the Local System to the Remote System, use the arrow pointing to the right. You can also select multiple files to download or upload using the Shift or Ctrl keys just as you would with any Windows file list.

The file you want to download in this lesson is eudor152.zip, which is located in the pub/micro/pc/win3/winsock directory. It is a popular shareware e-mail program called Eudora. You can use this file in Lesson 12, "Sending and Receiving E-Mail."

1. In the upper window of the Remote System, scroll down and double-click the pub folder (directory). Then select (in turn) the folders micro, pc, win3, and winsock.

2. When you're in the winsock folder, scroll down to eudor152.zip. Click once to highlight it.

3. Click the left pointing arrow between the two lists to download eudor152.zip from Gatekeeper to your PC. The downloaded file will be saved in the directory you specified during installation of WS_FTP32 LE. Figure 13.3 shows the Transfer Status window, showing the status of your file transfer. Depending on the size of the file and the speed of your Internet connection, the file can take anywhere from a few seconds to a few minutes to download. When you complete the download, WS_FTP32 stores the file in the folder that you last accessed on your Local System—which, by default, is the folder where the WS_FTP32 application program is stored.

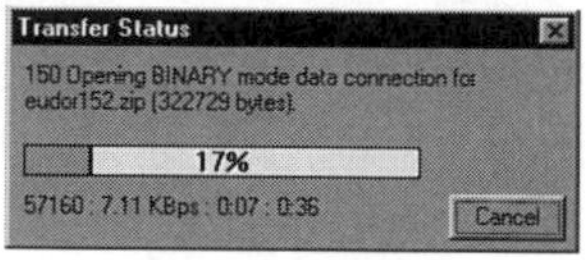

FIGURE 13.3   The status of a file being downloaded.

You may have noticed the three option buttons (ASCII, Binary, and Auto) near the bottom of the screen. They are used to set the transfer mode type. Binary is set by default, and for most transfers, you can leave it set to the Binary default. If you know the file you're transferring is purely text, you can use the ASCII mode. For more information on transfer mode, click WS_FTP's Help button and select Transferring Files.

> **Keep Your Files Together!** You'll find it convenient to
> create a subfolder within the folder where WS_FTP32 is
> stored, and use it to keep all of the files you download
> together. This helps keep your WS_FTP32 folder less
> cluttered.

4. When you finish downloading files, click the Exit button
    to log out of the FTP server and to exit WS_FTP32.

In this lesson, you learned how to use the Windows-based program WS_FTP32 to download files from an FTP server. In the
next lesson, you learn about viewing certain types of graphic
files commonly found on Web pages.

14 WORKING WITH NEWSGROUPS

In this lesson, you learn how UseNet newsgroups operate and how to read and post messages in newsgroups.

WHAT ARE USENET NEWSGROUPS?

UseNet newsgroups are nothing more than electronic discussion groups. In newsgroups, members usually limit their discussion to a single topic per group. More than 18,000 newsgroups exist, and topics range from aviation and alien visits to Zen and zoology.

> **UseNet** The term UseNet actually predates the Internet. UseNet refers to an early system of connecting mainframe computers to one another using ordinary telephone lines and crude versions of desktop modems to transmit and exchange research discussion articles.

Even though newsgroups are, by definition, oriented to single topics, as you browse through newsgroups, you'll notice that a single article in a topic can take many sides, or *threads*. Threads result from other users posting replies to the original article, and even the original author responding to some of the discussion on the original topic. Some newsreaders make it easy to follow threads, but be warned: threads have a way of veering off the original article's subject. As a rule, don't worry too much about following threads to the final reply.

Newsgroup members post messages that express their ideas and comments on the newsgroup topic. In most cases, newsgroups are neither censored nor moderated, but occasionally you will see a newsgroup where the administrator maintains a fairly strict policy concerning admittance of articles that do not directly pertain to the newsgroup subject. In these cases, the administrator deletes articles that aren't relevant to the discussion.

Members read and write additional messages about posted topics, either adding additional information or arguing with (or for that matter, agreeing with) the author of the original message. Posted messages may only remain in the newsgroup a few weeks, mainly because they occupy storage space. Your service provider manages newsgroups and will not want to tie up storage space longer than a few weeks. It is also up to your service provider to select the newsgroups. This explains why an Internet user in Portland, Oregon may not have access to the same newsgroups as a user in Annapolis, Maryland. If you hear of a newsgroup that is not carried by your provider, all you may need to do is simply ask the provider to add that group.

HOW ARE NEWSGROUPS ORGANIZED?

Newsgroups are organized into seven major categories:

alt (alternative)	Topics that fall outside of mainstream ideas and views; some can be very controversial.
comp (computers)	Topics associated with computers and computer science.
news (newsgroups)	News about newsgroups and their operation.
rec (recreational)	Topics that pertain to recreational interests.
sci (science)	Topics or areas of scientific interest.

| soc (social) | Topics or areas pertaining to social issues. |
| talk | Open subjects, with a focus on the aspects of a public debating forum. |

In addition to these seven major categories, many news servers also maintain a number of minor groups such as:

bionet (biology)	Issues and ideas centered around biology and the biological sciences.
biz (business)	Business-related topics.
courts	Court-related issues and events.
general	General interest topics not falling into any of the other groups.
humor	Humor, jokes, comedians, and so on.
misc. (miscellaneous)	Sometimes, just included to catch the overflow from general.

Newsgroups also tend to occasionally pop up around current issues or news topics, such as the OJ Simpson trial or the Oklahoma City bombing and trial. You can encounter countless other newsgroups. If you're inclined to want to make your ideas heard (or at least read), you should have no problem finding a forum in which to express your views.

You may also encounter newsgroups distinct to a certain region, such as skiing groups in the northern and western states, and beach topics along the southern coastal areas.

What You Need

If you're using Netscape as your browser, all you need is some basic information from your service provider, because Netscape has a built-in newsreader, or discussion reader as the company now likes to call it. You need to know the names of your news server and your mail server. If you're not using Netscape or if you want more functions than Netscape offers, you need a dedicated newsreader client program.

> **Newsreader**   A program you use to read and post
> articles to a newsgroup.

ACQUIRING AND SETTING UP YOUR NEWSREADER

If you're using Netscape as your browser, you can use its built-in newsreader capabilities. You can also use Internet Explorer 2.0 as a light-weight newsreader for casual viewing. However, if you're serious about getting involved with UseNet newsgroups, you should use a full-functioned newsreader. You can download a number of good ones from the Internet.

Free Agent is gaining in popularity and has all the features you're likely to need or want for maintaining the articles of the news-groups you subscribe to, for better control of keeping track of the articles you read and the articles you post. To download a copy, follow these steps:

1. Start your Web browser and enter **http://www.forteinc.com/forte/**, which takes you to Forté's Home Page shown in Figure 14.1. Forté is the manufacturer of Free Agent.

2. Click the Free Agent 1.11 link, and then follow the instructions on the download page (see Figure 14.2) to download Free Agent.

> **You Can Download Directly**   If you would rather use your FTP utility, you can download the file fa32-111.exe (the windows 95/NT 4.0 version) from one of these two FTP sites:
>
> **ftp.forteinc.com/pub/forte/free_agent/fa32-111.exe**
>
> **papa.indstate.edu/winsock-1/news/fa32-111.exe.**

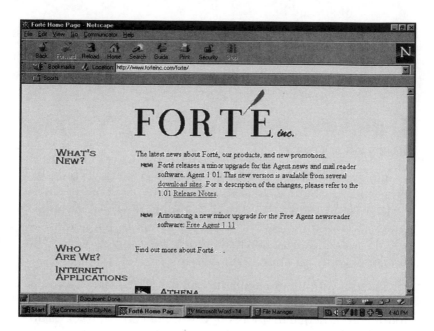

Figure 14.1   Forté's Home Page.

3. Run the file you downloaded, fa32-111.exe, to install Free Agent on your computer.

4. Double-click the Forté Agent icon to start Free Agent. When the program starts, it asks you to accept the license agreement. Read the agreement and click Accept.

5. Free Agent then prompts you to configure it to use your news server, mail server, e-mail address, name (optional), and time zone. You can get the names of the news server and the mail server from your service provider. Click OK to save the information you enter.

> **Configure from Netscape**   If you're using Netscape, and you were industrious enough (and ingenious enough) to enter news and mail information, you can transfer this information automatically to Free Agent by selecting the Use Information From Another Program button.

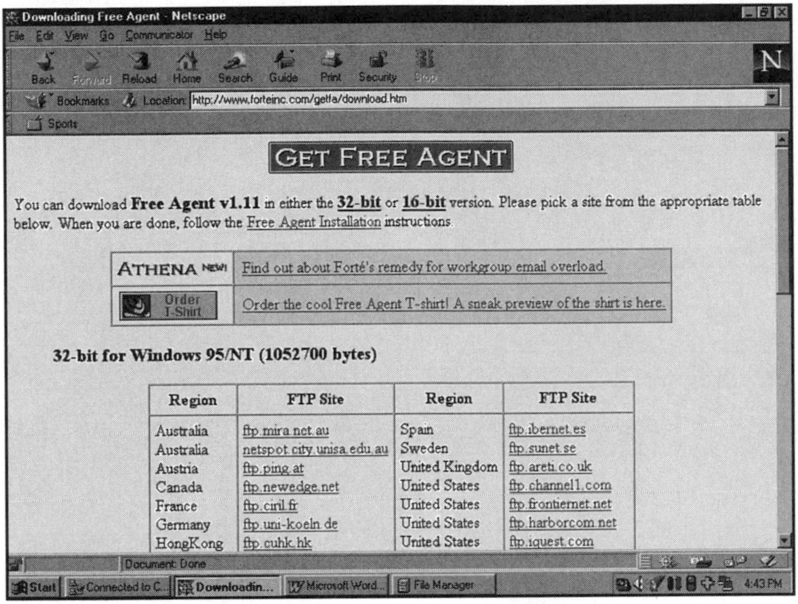

FIGURE 14.2   Find and download the Free Agent archive file.

READING NEWS ARTICLES

Once you configure your newsreader, it automatically attempts to connect to your news server to start getting newsgroup information:

1. Free Agent goes online to connect to your news server and get a complete listing of all newsgroups (see Figure 14.3). Click Yes to allow Free Agent to go online to get the complete listing of your news server's newsgroups. This takes anywhere from a few minutes to a half an hour or more, depending on the speed of your Internet connection.

2. When Free Agent displays the list of newsgroups it found on your news server, scroll down the displayed list and double-click on a newsgroup that interests you. The View Empty Group dialog box shown in Figure 14.4 appears.

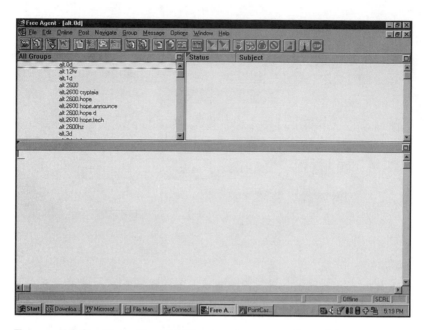

FIGURE 14.3 Free Agent with newsgroups gathered from your news server.

FIGURE 14.4 The View Empty Group dialog box.

3. To view all articles your news server has in this news-group, click the Get All Message Headers button. Keep in mind that some active newsgroups can have several hundred or even several thousand articles; displaying that many articles will take a few minutes. If you prefer to just

see a sampling of the articles available under a group, click the Sample 50 Article Headers button. After the articles are retrieved, they appear in a window.

4. To read an article, double-click its header (title). The article you clicked appears.

5. To read the threads associated with this article, select the View Next Unread Article in Thread icon. Free Agent displays the associated articles in the thread (see Figure 14.5).

> **Identifying Icons** To identify the icons in the Free Agent toolbar, use your mouse to place the pointer on one of the icons, but don't click. The icon's name, which is usually also a good indication of its function, appears.

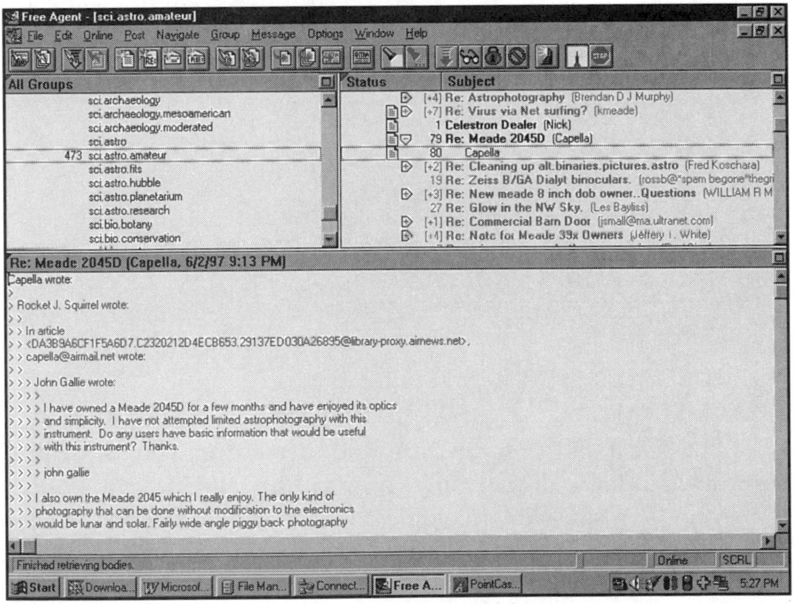

FIGURE 14.5 Associated articles in a thread.

SUBSCRIBING TO A NEWSGROUP

You don't have to subscribe to a newsgroup to read its articles or to post messages to it, but subscribing to newsgroups does have a few advantages. One major advantage is that you can set up your newsreader to display and update only the newsgroups you've subscribed to, as opposed to displaying the several hundred newsgroups carried by most news servers.

To subscribe to a newsgroup, follow these steps:

1. Scroll through the list of newsgroups found on your news server.

2. When you locate a newsgroup that interests you, click the group to highlight it, and then choose Group, Subscribe from the Free Agent menu bar. A small newspaper icon appears next to the newsgroup, as shown in Figure 14.6.

To unsubscribe to a group, repeat the previous steps. Note that the icon disappears, which indicates that you no longer subscribe to that newsgroup.

> **Another Way to Subscribe** Here's a slightly faster way to subscribe. Highlight the group and press Ctrl+S. You can also subscribe to a newsgroup by highlighting it and clicking the Subscribe icon.

DISPLAYING ONLY SUBSCRIBED-TO GROUPS

After you select all the groups you find interesting, you can adjust your newsreader to display only those groups. By displaying only the groups you subscribe to, you can select and update the articles in those groups without the tedium of scrolling through several hundred newsgroups.

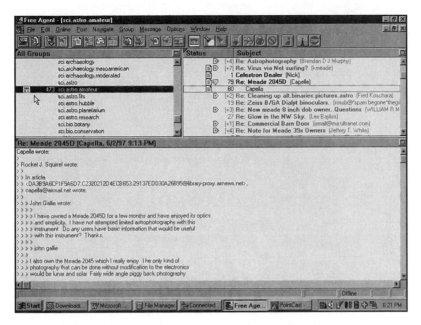

FIGURE 14.6   The newspaper icon marks a subscribed group.

To display only the groups to which you subscribe, choose Group, Show Only Subscribed Groups from the Free Agent menu bar. Figure 14.7 shows a window in which only the subscribed groups are displayed.

POSTING A NEWSGROUP ARTICLE

Reading the articles posted on the newsgroups you've subscribed to is only half the fun of being a newsgroup junkie. To fully appreciate the value of newsgroups, you have to post articles. Posting involves either responding to someone else's article or posting your own ideas.

While you're starting, I suggest that you stay away from the more "controversial" newsgroups, such as any involving sex, politics, Kennedy assassination theories, or anti-government conspiracies. Until you feel comfortable posting articles or responding to posted articles, try a few of the less controversial groups, such as rec.arts.disney-parks or alt.tv.game-shows.

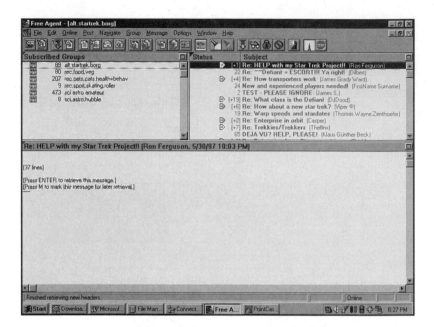

FIGURE 14.7 Free Agent displays only subscribed-to groups.

> **Post** To place an article that you write into the newsgroup for other users to read.

> **I'm Getting Hate Mail!** Sooner or later you will post an article that someone will absolutely disagree with, and they'll ask you if your brains are at the end of your digestive tract. This is called a *flame*. And if you post a completely off-the-wall comment, expect to get lots of flames. This is how newsgroup subscribers vehemently disagree.

To post a message, follow these steps:

1. Select a newsgroup on your news server and display the articles under it contained on your news server.

2. Select an article title that you know something about or can make a comment on.

3. Open the article so you can read it and so your follow-up (response) is properly formatted as a thread to that article.

4. Open the Post menu and choose Follow Up UseNet Message. When the follow-up window appears, enter your response under the article to which you are responding (see Figure 14.8).

 Follow-Up   Follow-up articles are also referred to as reader comments.

5. When you finish, select the Send Now or the Send Later button. (Lesson 12 covers sending and reading e-mail in detail.)

If you want to post a new article instead of responding to something written by someone else, open the Post menu (see step 3) and choose New UseNet Message.

The first few postings you do might seem a bit strange or awkward. After all, you're commenting on something created by a nameless and faceless entity.

Know Your Netiquette   While newsgroups are designed to promote the free discussion of ideas and issues, newsgroups are not a free-for-all, no-holds-barred, public soapbox. For a complete listing of Netiquette guidelines, go to the newsgroup located at news.announce.newusers and read (or better yet download) the article "Emily Postnews Answers Your Questions on Netiquette." You can also refer to Lesson 18, "Internet Etiquette."

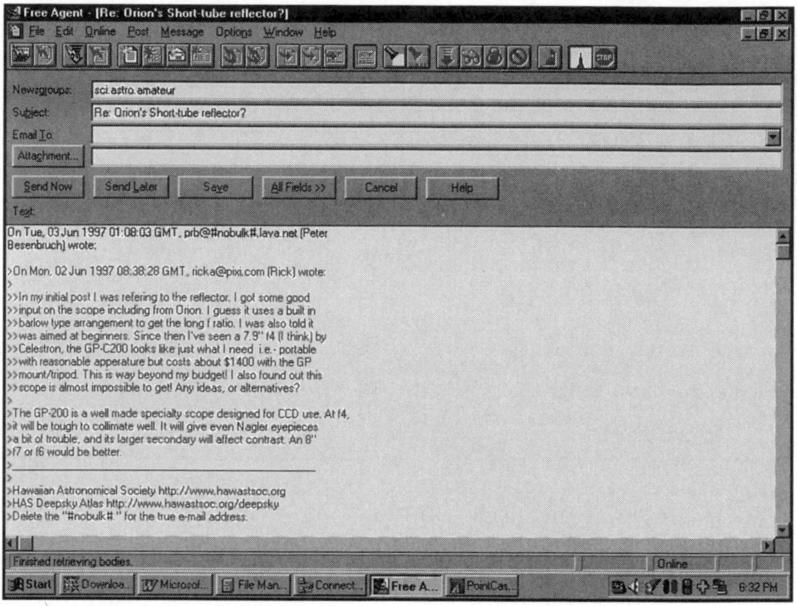

FIGURE 14.8   Create a follow-up to a posted article.

USING NETSCAPE OR INTERNET EXPLORER AS YOUR NEWSREADER

As I stated earlier, you can use either Netscape Navigator or Microsoft's Internet Explorer as your newsreader. Both will function well and may be easier to use and master, especially if you do not plan to turn the UseNet into a second career.

The application in the Netscape Communicator suite used as a newsreader is called Netscape Collabra, and is referred to as a "discussion group" reader. (So, if you are using Netscape Communicator, now you know why there is nothing there called newsreader.) Collabra does not have all of the bells and whistles you'll find in Free Agent (or the commercial version, Agent) but it will satisfy your needs if you are just an occasional newsgroup browser (see Figure 14.9).

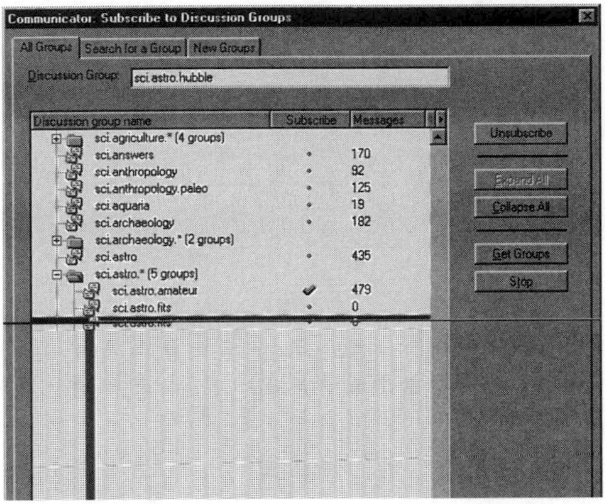

FIGURE 14.9   Netscape Collabra displaying newsgroups.

In this lesson, you learned how to subscribe to newsgroups and how to post articles. In the next lesson, you learn how to chat on the Internet.

REAL-TIME CHAT ON THE INTERNET

In this lesson, you learn about the two most popular types of Internet Chat—Internet Relay Chat and Web-based Chat—and how to set up and use chat programs for each.

WHAT IS INTERNET RELAY CHAT?

For some, Internet Relay Chat (or IRC) is the most enjoyable part of the Internet. As the name suggests, IRC is a means of "chatting" or having conversations with other Internet users in real-time. This means that both (or all) of you are sitting down chatting at the same time. You aren't actually talking to the other users. You're conducting your conversation by typing your questions and responses. In turn, you see the questions and responses typed by other users in your chat group, or chat room.

To chat, you need an IRC client—which is the software that enables you to connect to an IRC server—and an IRC server to connect to. There are more than 100 IRC servers running on the Internet.

IRC CLIENT SOFTWARE

You can download a number of good IRC client software programs from the Internet. If you want to try IRC chat, you can download a reasonably good chat client from **http://pebbles.axi.net/mirc/**—the mIRC Home Page.

The mIRC Home Page has both 16-bit and 32-bit versions for Windows. Follow the prompts to download the appropriate version and then run the downloaded file to install mIRC. Once the program has been installed, start mIRC and simply follow the prompts (again) to enter the needed configuration information and then connect to a chat server. The prompts make the procedure almost automatic.

Within about 10 minutes you should have mIRC up and running, and be connected to your first chat room (see Figure 15.1).

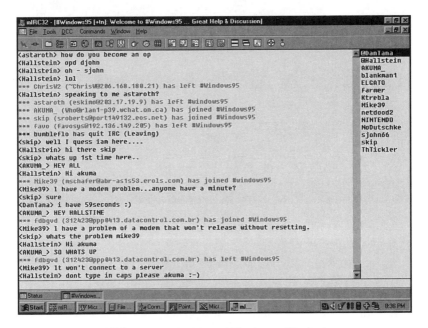

FIGURE 15.1   IRC connected to a Windows 95 chat room.

WEB-BASED CHAT

The World Wide Web has become the newest chat arena. And one of the most popular Web-based chat systems is ichat, located at **http://www.ichat.com/**.

To join an ichat chat room you need the ichat software which comes as either a Netscape plug-in or an Internet Explorer ActiveX client. Follow the prompts to ichat's download page and then select the appropriate program to download (see Figure 15.2).

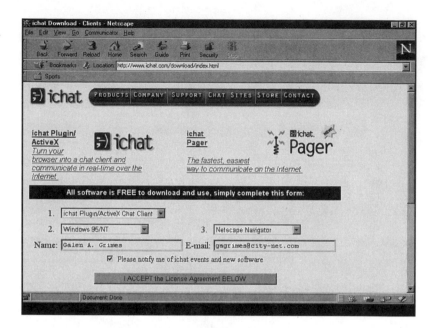

FIGURE 15.2   The ichat program download page.

After you download ichat, go ahead and install the program the same way you installed programs from other lessons. If you install the Netscape plug-in, remember to restart Netscape after the installation.

At the ichat Web site, there are numerous links to other Web sites which have already set up ichat chat rooms. One of the most prominent is a company you are probably already familiar with—Yahoo (see Figure 15.3).

To chat on the Yahoo chat site, you will be required to register. Follow the prompts to register, and in a few minutes you can take your pick of chat rooms and begin chatting.

If you find ichat an interesting way to spend time on the Internet, here is a list of a few other sites which have set up ichat chat rooms:

- JamTV (**http://www.jamtv.com/**)
- iVillage (**http://www.ivillage.com/**)

- Pathfinder (**http://www.pathfinder.com/chat**)
- Universal Studios (**http://chat.universalstudios.com:4080/**)
- Yahoo chat (**http://chat.yahoo.com**)
- Open 24 (**http://chat.open24.net:4080/**)

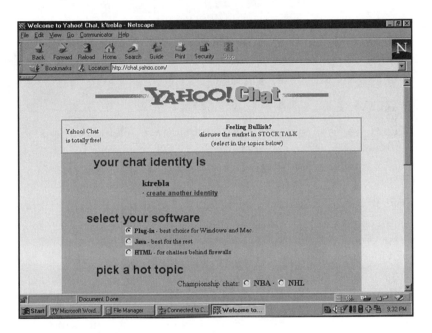

FIGURE 15.3   The Yahoo chat site.

In this lesson, you learned about Internet Relay Chat (IRC) and about two different IRC client programs: mIRC and ichat. In the next lesson, you learn how to use the Internet to make telephone calls.

16

LESSON

INTERNET TELEPHONES

In this lesson, you will learn about using the Internet to place telephone calls anywhere in the world.

WHAT YOU CAN REALLY EXPECT FROM INTERNET PHONES

Despite the headlines you've read about the challenges various Baby Bells have made against the use of "unregulated" Internet Phone products, Ma Bell is not shaking in her boots about the proliferation of a dozen or more products that let you conduct "free phone" calls over the Internet.

Let's begin by separating fact from fiction. It is true you can use these products to talk to virtually anyone, anywhere in the world, provided that person also has a computer using the same or a compatible Internet phone product. And you can make "free phone" calls, provided you have purchased a computer, a sound card, a microphone, speakers, and an Internet connection. Those free phone calls can have a startup cost of around a thousand dollars.

But if you already happen to have a computer connected to the Internet, and you also happen to have a sound card along with the usual accompanying accouterments (microphone and speakers), then all you need is the right software and you can begin talking to friends and acquaintances who have similar setups.

IS IT REALLY THAT SIMPLE?

To be perfectly honest, no it isn't. But after you complete this lesson you'll be a lot closer to making an Internet phone work than you were before. Making an Internet phone work is not rocket science, but it does take a bit of careful work, and sometimes some luck as you will soon see.

How Good Is the Sound Quality?

How good your sound quality is depends on a lot of factors—how good your sound card and speakers are, the speed of your Internet connection, and most importantly, the software you use to make your Internet phone calls. Some products do a reasonably good job of transmitting the human voice over the Internet. You won't get CD-quality sound, but you can get decent phone quality sound. On the other hand, some Internet phone products will make you sound like you're calling from a cheap phone during a thunderstorm from the bottom of a cave. Fortunately, there are at least a half a dozen Internet phone products you can try for nothing more than the time it takes to download the product from a Web site. Fortunately too, you are reading a book written by someone who has already downloaded and tried a half dozen or so products so you won't have to.

TeleVox By Voxware

One of the first products you should try is TeleVox by Voxware, Inc. Voxware makes a commercial product you can purchase, but also allows you to sample the goods before you buy. You can download a fully functional copy of TeleVox, which you can use for 14 days.

TeleVox produces about the best quality audio you will find of all of the Internet phone products and is fairly easy to setup and use. Let's download and install a copy of TeleVox so you can judge for yourself:

1. If you haven't started Netscape already, go ahead and login to your local service provider and start Netscape or IE4.

2. Head for the Voxware site at **http://www.voxware.com** (see Figure 16.1).

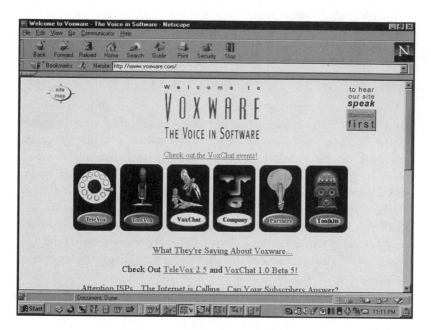

Figure 16.1   The Voxware Web site, home of TeleVox.

3. Follow the prompts to download TeleVox version 2.5. You will be required to register, but then afterwards you will be allowed to download a 14-day trial copy.

Limited Availability   TeleVox is currently only available for Windows 95/NT. But if are using another operating system, stay tuned. At the end of this lesson I will give you names of companies which produce Internet phone products available for Windows 3.1 and the Apple Mac.

4. When the download is completed, run the program you downloaded to install TeleVox on your computer (see Figure 16.2).

5. When the installation is completed, you can start TeleVox by clicking the TeleVox 2.5 icon. The first time you run TeleVox, the setup Wizard will run to help you configure TeleVox for your system. The Wizard will take you

through several screens where you can enter information about yourself which will appear on the Voxware directories, and conduct several tests on your computer's sound system to help you set input and output sound levels. When the setup Wizard is completed, the main TeleVox user interface is displayed on your screen (see Figure 16.3).

FIGURE. 16.2   Installing TeleVox 2.5 under Windows 95.

6. To place a call select the Call button and the Call dialog box appears displaying the Voxware directory (see Figure 16.4).

7. Select a user from the list and click the Dial button to place your call. You should hear a dial tone and then you should hear TeleVox ringing the person you are attempting to call.

I Don't Hear Anything!   If you don't hear the dial tone and then the ringing signal, check to make sure the volume is turned up on your speakers. If you still don't hear anything, rerun the Setup Wizard from the Help menu and recheck the settings for your computer and sound system.

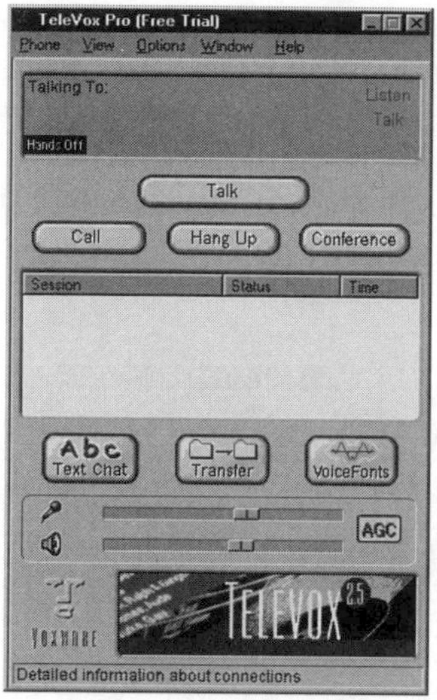

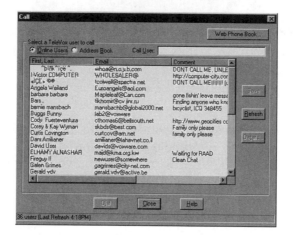

FIGURE 16.3   The main TeleVox user interface.

FIGURE 16.4   The Voxware directory of TeleVox users.

8. When the person you are calling answers, simply begin talking into your microphone to begin your conversation.

Don't be disappointed if the first few times you attempt a conversation the sound is somewhat distorted. Occasionally, you will have to adjust your audio settings (select Options, Preferences, Audio) before the sound is optimal. One nice feature built into TeleVox is that if you can't make the audio work just the way you want it, you can always select the ABC Text Chat button and converse with the other party just the same as you would in a chat room.

In addition to making Internet phone calls, TeleVox also allows you to make conference calls, and exchange files.

OTHER INTERNET PHONE PRODUCTS TO TRY

If TeleVox doesn't do it for you, another Internet phone product you might want to try is VocalTec. You can download a trial copy of VocalTec from the VocalTec Web site at **http://www.vocaltec.com** (see Figure 16.5).

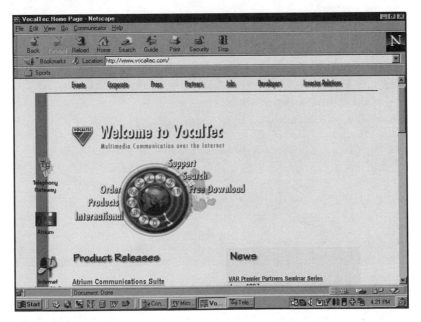

FIGURE 16.5   The VocalTec Web site.

VocalTec's audio quality is very good, but in my humble opinion, it is not quite as good as the quality produced by TeleVox. But VocalTec does produce versions of its phone application for Windows 3.1 and the Mac.

Intel, the company which produces the majority of computer microprocessors, also makes an Internet phone product. The Intel Internet Video phone is primarily geared at video transmissions over the Internet but will also reproduce audio alone if you are lacking a video camera. You can download and try a copy at **http://connectedpc.com/iaweb/cpc/iivphone/ index.htm**.

Still another Internet phone product worth taking a look at, or a listen to, is FreeTel, which you can download from the FreeTel Web site at **http://www.freetel.com** (see Figure 16.6).

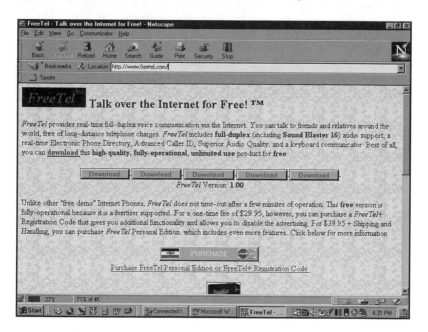

FIGURE 16.6   The FreeTel Web site.

In this lesson, you learned how to make free phone calls over the Internet and got to try a few Internet phone products. In the next lesson, you will learn about push technology and one of the premier push technology products, PointCast.

POINTCAST AND PUSH TECHNOLOGY

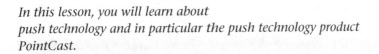

In this lesson, you will learn about push technology and in particular the push technology product PointCast.

WHAT IS PUSH TECHNOLOGY?

The Web browser components in Netscape Communicator and Microsoft's Internet Explorer 4.0 use what is called *pull technology*. When you use Navigator or IE4, you point the browser at a particular Web page and the browser "pulls" the contents of the page down to your computer and displays on your screen the information you are interested in seeing. You only see the information contained on the Web pages you explicitly request.

Push technology is somewhat different. Instead of you requesting specific information and *pull*-ing the information down to your computer, a Web server will periodically *push* information down to your computer which you can later view. Think of it this way: pull technology is similar to you going to a newsstand and buying a newspaper. You have to initiate the action and you might only go every other day or just once a week. Push technology, in turn, is like having the newspaper delivered to your front door every morning. You don't have to initiate any action to have information delivered to you.

WHAT IS POINTCAST AND HOW DOES IT WORK?

PointCast was one of the first push technology products on the market and is still one of the first to come to mind when the topic of push technology is discussed. PointCast supplies U.S. and world news (see Figure 17.1), sports (see Figure 17.2), business information (see Figure 17.3), and lifestyle and health information.

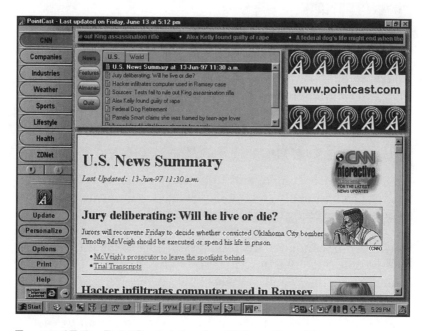

FIGURE 17.1   PointCast delivering U.S. and world news.

GETTING YOUR COPY OF POINTCAST

PointCast is free to download from the PointCast Web site:

1. Start your Web browser, either Netscape Navigator or Internet Explorer 4, and head for the PointCast Web site at **http://www.pointcast.com/** (see Figure 17.4).

2. Select the download link (there are several download links, so take your pick) and follow the prompts to download the PointCast client.

3. After you complete the download, run the installation file (program) you just downloaded to install the PointCast client on your computer.

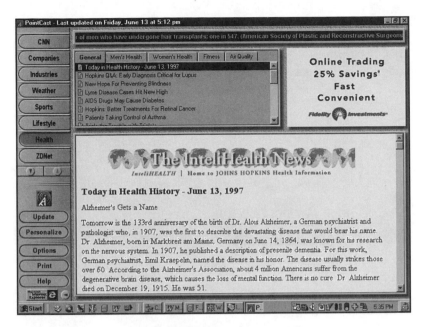

FIGURE 17.2   PointCast delivering business information.

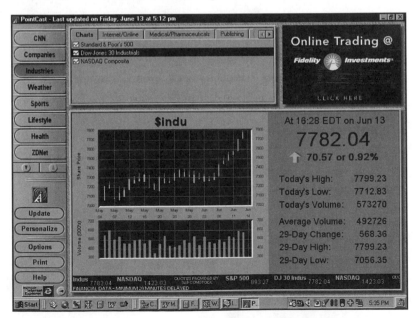

FIGURE 17.3   PointCast delivering business information.

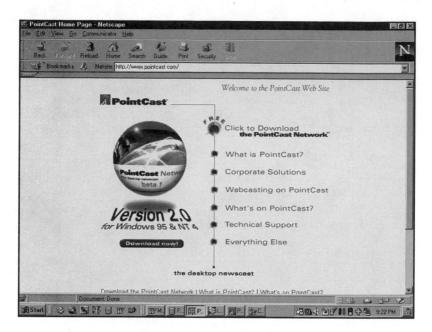

FIGURE 17.4   The PointCast Web site.

4. At the end of the installation, select Personalize PointCast so you can configure PointCast to deliver the type of information you want to view.

5. If you use a dial-in connection for the Internet, select your dialer at the first screen. If are using Windows 95, select the Windows 95 dialer. You can also optionally configure the connection PointCast will use. And if you want to select an external browser, either Netscape or IE4, select the Use External Browser check box and then locate the directory where you have installed either Netscape or IE4. Select OK to continue.

6. When the Personalize the PointCast Network dialog box appears (see Figure 17.5) make sure the Channels sheet is displayed. If this sheet is not displayed select the Channels tab.

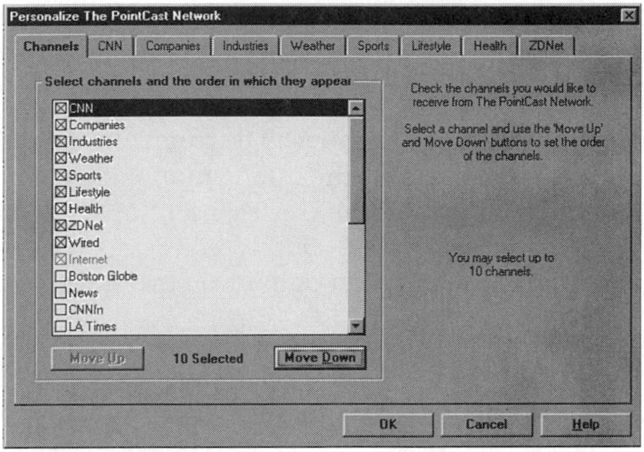

Figure 17.5   The Channels sheet in the Personalize the PointCast Network dialog box.

7. Select as many of the sheets in the Personalize the PointCast Network dialog box as you like, and select as many of the channels or types of information you want PointCast to deliver to your computer. When you complete your configuration, select OK to close the dialog box and save your configuration settings.

> **Channels**   Companies that push information to your computer using the PointCast client application. Some of the channels available through PointCast include CNN, the Wall Street Journal, Chicago Tribune, and the Boston Globe.

8. The next screen will prompt you to perform your first update. Go ahead and select Update to begin having PointCast push the first batch of information to your computer. The first update will take a few minutes to complete. The length of time will depend on how fast your Internet connection is and how much information you selected to have PointCast push to your computer.

It's also a good idea to keep your first batch of information small until you are accustomed to how long each update will take.

9. In a few minutes the update will be completed and you can begin browsing over the information PointCast has delivered to your computer (see Figure 17.6).

There is one more configuration option you may want to change:

1. On the main PointCast interface, select the Options button to open the Options dialog box.

2. Select the Update tab to display the update sheet (see Figure 17.7). On the Update sheet select how often you want PointCast to update the information it is supplying to you. If you are using a dial-in connection, it is best to select to update your information only when you select Update.

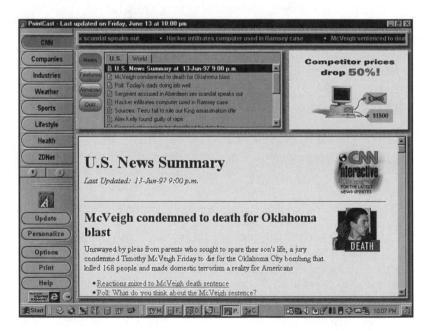

FIGURE 17.6 PointCast after its first information update.

OTHER PUSH TECHNOLOGY PRODUCTS

PointCast is by no means the only push technology application currently available to you. Both Netscape and Microsoft offer push technology applications in their Web browser suites— Netscape gives you Netcaster (see Figure 17.7) and Microsoft gives you its IE4 Active Desktop.

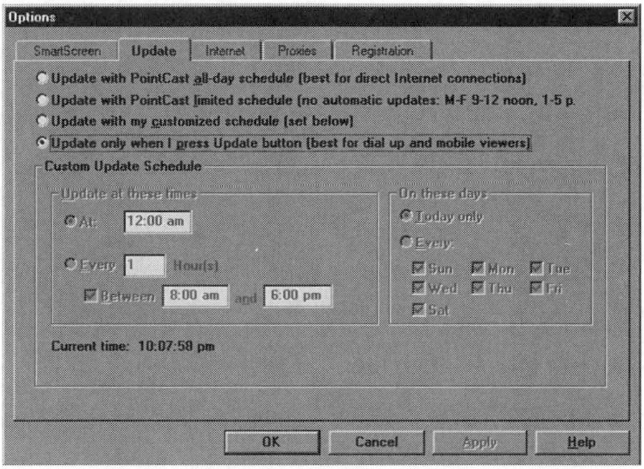

FIGURE 17.7   The Update sheet on the Options dialog box.

Both IBM and Yahoo have push technology products in the form of a news ticker which you can set to constantly update you with news headlines (see Figure 17.9) .

In this lesson, you learned about PointCast and other push technology products. In the next lesson, you will learn about Internet etiquette.

FIGURE 17.8   Netscape's push technology product Netcaster.

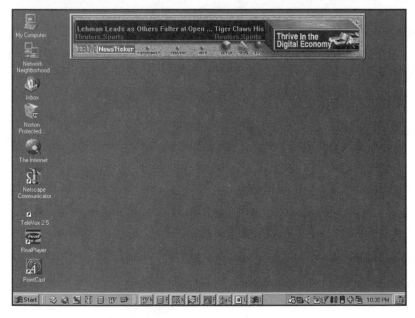

FIGURE 17.9   The IBM News ticker.

INTERNET ETIQUETTE

In this lesson, you learn netiquette: the proper Internet protocol to use when interacting with other Internet users.

WHEN NETIQUETTE COMES INTO PLAY

Sitting alone in front of your computer surfing the Net, it may not have dawned on you that there is also an Internet protocol for interacting with other Internet users. Internet etiquette, or netiquette, is a set of written and unwritten rules that you are expected to learn and abide by. Depending on how you spend your time on the Internet, it is possible that you may rarely encounter other users. It is also possible to have numerous encounters each and every time you log in. The three primary areas where netiquette will most often come into play are:

- E-mail
- Newsgroups
- Chat rooms

Each of these areas has its own set of rules, and whether you follow these rules or trample all over them can mean the difference between amicable interaction and flame wars. If you're not familiar with the Internet term flame, you will be by the time you finish this lesson.

Remember too, that the information presented in this lesson is not all-inclusive. You should treat this information as a general guideline, not as the 10 Commandments for Internet Etiquette.

E-MAIL AND ITS CODE OF CONDUCT

You may not think there is much that can go wrong using e-mail. After all, you simply write a message and then send it to someone. What could be simpler? Here is a short list of DOs and DON'Ts associated with this seemingly harmless act.

DO...

- Be considerate of others; keep your messages short and to the point. E-mail is for sending messages, not dissertations. How do you like reading long, rambling e-mail messages?

- Use smileys or emoticons such as :-) and :-(to express yourself in e-mail, but use them sparingly. These funny little symbols can convey the tone of a message and prevent someone from taking it in a different way than you meant it. For more information on emoticons, see the following Web pages:

    http://www.epages.com/~rhubarbs/faces.htm

    http://www.jsp.umontreal.ca/~chantane/fra/texts/emoticon.txt

    http://peaksnewsnet.com/internet/internet5.html

- Keep signature files short (no more than one or two lines). Many users have adopted the habit of adding bits or irony or witty sayings called signatures to the end of their e-mail messages. Many e-mail programs allow you to create a list of signature files, which they append to the end of your messages. Some examples include:

    "You can make it idiot-proof, but they'll just keep making better idiots."

    "I used to be indecisive, but now I'm not sure."

    "Power no longer consists of knowledge but in functioning as a link between bodies of knowledge." (Jean-Marie Guehenno, The End of the Nation State)

"At 26, the Internet is older than most of its users."
(George Conrades, CEO of BBN)

DON'T...

- USE ALL CAPITALS IN YOUR MESSAGES! Because e-mail messages are read and not heard, you don't have the opportunity to express yourself as you would if you were using a telephone. ALL CAPITALS is the e-mail equivalent of SHOUTING!

- Send junk mail! The only thing more annoying than emptying junk out of the mailbox at your front door is emptying junk mail out of your e-mail mailbox. Most users find it annoying, and it only adds to the congestion on the Internet.

- Send an e-mail message you would not want to read to your mother, or hear read on the evening news. While this may sound strange, the message here is, don't put embarrassing information in your e-mail messages.

PROPER CONDUCT IN NEWSGROUPS

Rules of conduct on newsgroups are usually spelled out for you, and if you plan to spend much time in newsgroups, especially if you plan to post messages, you would be wise to download and read the newsgroup FAQs (Frequently Asked Questions) before you become an active participant. You can usually find rules and netiquette info in the newsgroup **news.announce.newusers**.

The news.announce.newusers newsgroup contains these rules and many others that you need to follow when you're in newsgroups:

- Insulting, degrading, and racist comments are forbidden.

- Keep your postings short and succinct, especially when quoting someone else's message or when responding to another user's posting.

- Don't post personal messages. If you need to send a personal message, use e-mail.

- Don't try to conduct business or try to solicit customers in newsgroups.

USING ABBREVIATIONS

In trying to keep messages short and clear, a common practice you'll see in newsgroups, e-mail, and chat rooms is the use of abbreviations for commonly used terms. Using abbreviations is one place where using ALL CAPS is acceptable. Below are some you will likely encounter:

Abbreviation	Meaning
BTW	by the way
IMHO	in my humble opinion
OTOH	on the other hand
TTYL	talk to you later
LOL	laughing out loud
ROTFL	rolling on the floor laughing
RTFM	read the f—ing manual
FYI	for your information

GETTING FLAMED

Sooner or later, you will encounter the term flame, especially if you spend a lot of time in newsgroups. A *flame* is a sharp retort or criticism to a posting or comment that users consider particularly stupid or irrelevant. You can also get flamed by committing a major breach of netiquette. As a new user, you are sometimes spared because many veteran users expect as much from newbies, as new users are called. But not all veterans are patient, so be forewarned.

IT GETS MORE PERSONAL IN CHAT ROOMS

Chat rooms are conversations in real time, so most of the same rules of protocol and behavior you would use when talking with a small group in a social setting, such as a party, usually apply in chat rooms as well.

Keep in mind, too, that some chat rooms, because of the nature of the topics (in adult rooms, for example) being discussed, may impose their own set of rules and behavior about what type of language is permitted.

In general, here are some of the basic guidelines you should be aware of:

- Say hello when you enter a room. It's considered polite to offer a short greeting, but don't turn this into an overture.

- Use a nickname. Chat rooms are by definition informal, so pick a nickname. Also, if you plan on doing the chat circuit on a regular basis, use the same nickname so others can become familiar with you.

- Don't use all caps. Remember, it's LIKE SHOUTING AT SOMEONE!!!

- Don't repeatedly ask the same question if it appears you are being ignored. You may think you are making a witty contribution to the conversation, but others may not.

- If you use abbreviations, don't deviate from the norm. It's very frustrating for others to see you make some relevant comment, only to have it followed up with some indecipherable jumble of letters.

Obviously, there are going to be some rules we have missed here, but in general, these should at least help you to start in the worlds of e-mail, newsgroups, and IRC chat. If you ever have any questions about what is proper etiquette or protocol, common sense and courtesy should get you through most situations.

In this lesson, you learned about Internet etiquette. In the next lesson, you will learn how to select an Internet service provider.

SELECTING AN INTERNET SERVICE PROVIDER

In this lesson, you learn how to select an Internet Service Provider (ISP).

WHAT IS INTERNET SERVICE?

Internet access comes in a variety of connection choices and account types, as you will soon see, depending on who provides the service and what hardware and software you use. This lesson examines the service options available to users with stand-alone computers, rather than the options available to users who have Internet access through a local area network (LAN).

> **Stand-Alone Computer** A computer that is not directly connected to another computer or computer system, such as a local area network. To access other computers, users with stand-alone computers usually use a modem to connect over ordinary telephone lines.

YOU CAN GET ACCESS THROUGH YOUR ONLINE SERVICE

Many of the commercial online services, such as CompuServe, America Online, Prodigy, and now The Microsoft Network, offer Internet access. Internet access through these services is usually quick and easy to set up. The downside to using a commercial online service used to be that the meter was constantly running every minute you were connected. But now most of the online services have adopted a flat rate fee structure in order to compete head-to-head with the legion of Internet service providers who had been luring away their customer base.

Of course, now there is a new downside to using a commercial online service—getting access! The chief complaint many of the online services hear now is that "it is next to impossible to get through," and that users attempting to dial-in almost always get a busy signal.

Commercial online service providers counter with the argument that they offer a wide array of additional services (vendor forums, e-mail, file/program downloading, chat rooms, and so on) all neatly organized and easily accessed through a familiar or easy-to-learn interface. However, once you become familiar with the Internet, you will find that most, if not all, of these services are available at a fraction of the cost. You only need to know where to look.

The questions here are, "What is access like in my location?", "How much time will I spend on the Internet each month?" and "Is it worth it to have these services laid out for me in a nice, neat little package?"

ABOUT INTERNET SERVICE PROVIDER SHELL ACCOUNTS

Most Internet service providers have abandoned shell accounts, but these accounts are still available—usually at rock-bottom prices. Shell accounts are cheap because they are text-only. In a world of graphical user interfaces (GUIs) and multimedia razzle-dazzle, few users are satisfied with surfing the Net with a text-only view.

On the plus side, a text-only interface does have one major advantage—speed! When you eliminate pictures, graphical fonts, and colors, you can access the Internet very quickly. In previous lessons, you saw how you could turn off the graphics mode at times when you want to surf the Net at "warp speed" instead of cruising on "impulse power."

WHAT ARE INTERNET SERVICE PROVIDER SLIP/PPP ACCOUNTS?

Serial Line Internet Protocol (SLIP) and Point-to-Point Protocol (PPP) are two types of Internet accounts most users presently turn to. SLIP is the older of the two types of Internet connections explained here. As its name implies, SLIP allows you to connect to a service provider over a serial communication line, such as a telephone line. Developed after SLIP, PPP is also serial in nature, but it provides a higher degree of error detection and compression in its connection to your service provider. When given a choice, choose PPP.

Still relatively inexpensive in most areas (especially compared to commercial networks), these accounts offer you Internet access through graphical interfaces and allow you to experience the full depth of the Internet and its services. One of the goals of this book is to show you how to set up SLIP and PPP accounts. That information begins in Lesson 19.

Error Detection   A feature that detects errors between the source and recipient and tells the source to resend the communications signal. Error detection is built into PPP connections, but SLIP connections get error detection from an outside source—often hardware. Today's higher speed modems assist by providing extra error detection, too.

Compression   The encoding of communication signals so they can be sent as shorter signals, which take less time to send.

SELECTING AN INTERNET SERVICE PROVIDER

Now that you know something about the types of Internet accounts available, you need to know how to go about selecting an Internet service provider. Don't attempt to make the determination solely on the basis of price. Read through the following questions, consider which of the service options are important to you, and discuss them with potential service providers.

- Is the call to your ISP a local call? The whole idea is to keep your costs to a minimum, which means avoiding long distance or toll telephone charges.

- Do you charge a flat rate, or by the minute/hour? Flat-rate providers are becoming more common, but many providers keep the meter running and charge you by the hour. Some hourly rate providers give you a minimum number of hours before the meter starts. Some give you as few as 3 hours per day, while others give you as many as 100 hours per month.

- Do you offer shell, SLIP, or PPP accounts? PPP is the best type of connectivity for your money.

- How many incoming telephone lines do you make available? The least expensive provider is not a bargain if all you get when you dial in is a busy signal.

- What communication speeds do you offer? You set your modem to this speed to communicate with your provider's modems. Hardly any service providers offer speeds less than 14,400 bits per second (bps). If you're using a modem with a top speed of 28,800bps, make sure your provider has phone lines that talk to your modem at this speed. If you think you might upgrade to ISDN connections sometime in the future, inquire as to whether your provider can support these connections.

- Do you offer e-mail, newsgroups, and an online chat service? Can you browse the World Wide Web and send and receive files through FTP? Can you use Telnet and Gopher? In previous lessons, you learned about these capabilities and what you can do with them. These are all basic Internet services that your service provider should offer.

> **ISDN**   Integrated Services Digital Network. The modems you use now communicate by converting the digital signal from your computer to an analog signal. In other words, your modem converts bits and bytes to sound and then transmits this analog signal over standard telephone lines. ISDN communicates as a digital signal, which means it does not use a "standard" modem, and thus is a lot faster (because the signal doesn't have to be converted).

A service provider should offer at least those services listed in the preceding list. Some service providers go further and make shareware software and technical support available.

If you're wondering how to find an Internet provider, look for ads in online magazines, check the yellow pages, or simply ask someone about his or her provider.

Also, if you want to "sample the goods," many state-run universities have started providing Internet-access terminals in student union buildings and libraries where anyone can literally walk in off the street and get on the Internet. Some colleges and universities are also providing for their students standard, dial-up Internet accounts having recognized the Internet's potential as a valuable research source.

In this lesson, you learned what questions to ask when shopping for an Internet service provider and what services your service provider should offer. In the next three lessons, you will learn how to configure your PC to access the Internet whether you are using Windows 95, Windows 3.1, or the Apple Macintosh.

CONFIGURATION FOR WINDOWS 3.1 USERS

In this lesson, you will learn how to configure Windows 3.1 to connect to the Internet using a dial-up connection.

WHAT YOU WILL NEED

There are more than a dozen Internet kits you can buy that allow you to log in to the Internet while running Windows 3.1. You can save a few dollars by picking up a few utilities and manually configuring Windows 3.1 as your Internet client.

The three utilities you will need are:

- A Winsock program

- A dialer

- An FTP utility

A Winsock, short for Windows Sockets, is the RFC-2091 specification (Internet specification) designed to ensure compatibility between multiple TCP/IP product vendors. The Winsock for Windows 3.1 is implemented in winsock.dll. There are numerous ways to load your Winsock. This lesson discusses a shareware product called Trumpet Winsock.

A dialer is simply a Winsock-compliant program used to dial into your Internet service provider. In this lesson, the dialer used is also Trumpet Winsock.

While an FTP utility is not essential for connecting to the Internet, you will find it helpful to have one so that you can download other Internet programs you will need once you set up Windows 3.1.

CONFIGURING TRUMPET WINSOCK

Most Internet service providers will also supply you with Trumpet Winsock and an FTP utility as part of your connection package. Follow these steps to install Trumpet Winsock:

1. Create a directory for the program, using the directory name \TRUMPET. You can either use Windows File Manager or the **MKDIR \TRUMPET** command at the DOS prompt.

2. Copy all of the files into the \TRUMPET directory. Again you can use File Manager or the COPY *.* command at the DOS prompt.

3. Open your AUTOEXEC.BAT file and add the **\TRUMPET** directory at the end of the PATH statement. Then reboot your PC so that the newly configured PATH statement takes effect.

4. Start Windows and start Trumpet Winsock by double-clicking the TCPMAN.EXE program in the **\TRUMPET** directory. Figure 20.1 shows the opening screen of Trumpet Winsock and the fields for which you will supply information.

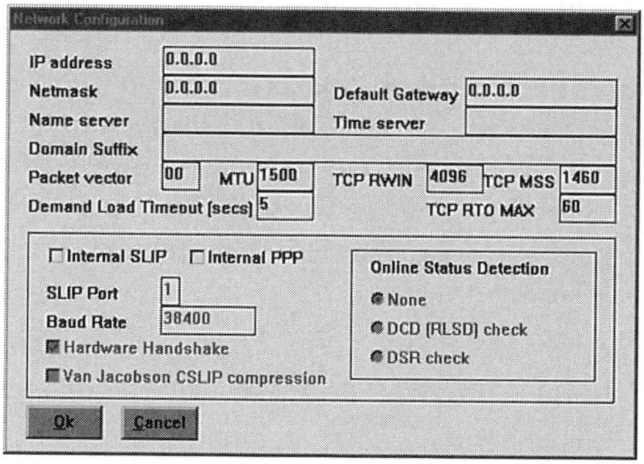

FIGURE 20.1   The Trumpet Winsock main screen.

5. Select Internal SLIP or Internal PPP, depending on which type of connection you have with your service provider.

6. Fill in the IP addresses for your PC's IP address, netmask, name server, default gateway, and domain suffix. You can get all of this information from your service provider. Find out whether your ISP assigns you a static IP address (which means you use the same IP address every time you log in) or a dynamic IP address (which could be different each time you log in).

7. Enter the communications port (COM1, COM2, and so on) your modem is connected to, and the speed of your modem (14,400 or 28,800, for example).

8. Click OK to save your entries, and Trumpet Winsock displays your settings, which might look similar to those displayed in Figure 20.2.

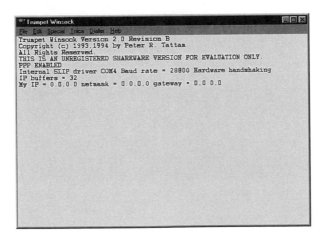

FIGURE 20.2   Trumpet Winsock displays your connection parameters.

9. Open the Dialler menu and choose Edit scripts. Full instructions for editing the sample scripts are supplied in a readme file in your \TRUMPET directory.

After you finish editing the sample scripts, you are ready to test your configuration. Go back to the Dialler menu to test your connection. Follow the instructions given you by your provider for logging into your provider's system. If your connection fails, go back and check all of your entries to make sure they match the information given to you by your provider.

Once you successfully log in to your provider's system, you can use the FTP utility supplied by your service provider to start downloading additional Internet utilities you will need or want (such as a Web browser, an e-mail program, Gopher program, and so on). If you're given a choice, make sure you download the 16-bit version compatible with Windows 3.1.

In this lesson, you learned how to configure Windows 3.1 to connect to the Internet. In the next lesson, you will learn how to configure Windows 95 so you can use it to connect to the Internet.

CONFIGURATION FOR WINDOWS 95 USERS

*In this lesson, you learn how to set up
your Windows 95 Internet connection using the Internet Wizard in
Microsoft Plus!.*

INSTALLING MICROSOFT PLUS!

Microsoft Plus! is an add-on product for Windows 95 that gives
you system- and disk-maintenance tools, desktop-enhancement
products, Internet support, and a really cool pinball game. Before
you can use the Internet Setup Wizard, you have to install
Microsoft Plus!.

> **You Can Also Use the Internet Jumpstart Kit!** Many
> dealers substitute the "free" Internet Jumpstart Kit as an
> alternative to MS Plus! for users who want access to the
> Internet. If the Jumpstart Kit is not included with your PC,
> ask your dealer or your ISP for it.

> **For PPP Only** The Internet Setup Wizard only works for
> PPP (Point-to-Point Protocol) connections. But if your copy
> of Windows 95 came on CD, look in the /Admin/Apptools/
> Dscript folder for information on setting up a SLIP connec-
> tion.

If you haven't installed Microsoft Plus!, go ahead and insert the
CD or disk into the appropriate drive and follow the installation

instructions. After you've installed it, look over Table 21.1, which lists the information you need to get from your provider so you can enter it when you run the Setup Wizard.

TABLE 21.1   INFORMATION YOUR INTERNET SERVICE PROVIDER SHOULD SUPPLY

INFORMATION	DEFINITION
Domain Server or IP Address	The provider's 12-digit IP address (nnn.nnn.nnn.nnn); each segment value is in the range 0–255.
Subnet Mask	Another 12-digit address in the form nnn.nnn.nnn.nnn.
Domain Name	Your provider's domain name, in the form provider.com or provider.net.
Host Name	If used (some providers tell you to leave this blank), your provider supplies it.
Mail Server Name	Your e-mail server's domain name.
News Server Name	Your newsgroup server's domain name.
E-mail Address	Your e-mail address in the form username@mailserver.
Commands used to log in to ISP	Commands such as "Enter user name and password" and any subsequent commands you need to follow to log in to the provider.
Type of IP address (dynamic or static)	Your provider assigns you a permanent IP address to use if it's static.
Dial-Up phone	The phone number you dial to number connect to your provider.

RUNNING THE INTERNET SETUP WIZARD

The Internet Setup Wizard is found on the Internet Tools menu under Accessories. In this lesson, you will see step-by-step how to supply the information the Setup Wizard needs to create your Internet connection. Remember, your use of the Internet Setup Wizard will differ if you use a different provider and connect from a different city.

To start the Internet Setup Wizard, follow these steps:

1. Select the Start button on the taskbar and choose Programs, Accessories, Internet Tools, and Internet Setup Wizard (see Figure 21.1).

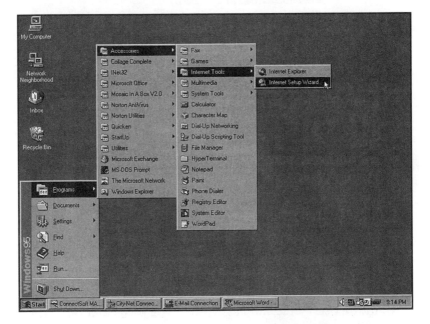

FIGURE 21.1   The menu path to Internet Setup Wizard.

2. At the opening screen, click the Next> button to begin. If your modem is not already set up, Windows 95 prompts you to set up your modem.

3. In the How to Connect dialog box, click the I already
   have an account with a different service provider option
   button as shown in Figure 21.2. Then click the Next>
   button.

FIGURE 21.2   Installing Internet support with your own ISP
(Internet service provider).

4. In the Service Provider Information dialog box, enter the
   name of your Internet service provider. This is just a label
   that identifies the shortcut icon you will use to connect
   to your provider. It can be anything you like. Click the
   Next> button to continue.

5. In the Phone Number dialog box, enter the phone number of your provider. Even if you're dialing a local number, enter the area code and country code (select the
   correct code from the Country Code drop-down list).
   Finally, select the Bring up terminal window after dialing
   check box. You will use the terminal window to log in to
   your ISP (see Figure 21.3). Click the Next> button to continue.

6. In the User Name and Password dialog box, enter the
   login name (user name) and password set up for you by
   your provider. (Even though you enter your user name
   and password here, some login systems by some providers
   will not accept these unless you also type them in the
   terminal window.) Click the Next> button to continue.

FIGURE 21.3   Supply your provider's phone number.

7. In the IP Address dialog box, select how you get your user IP address. Your provider should supply you with this information (see Figure 21.4). Click the Next> button to continue.

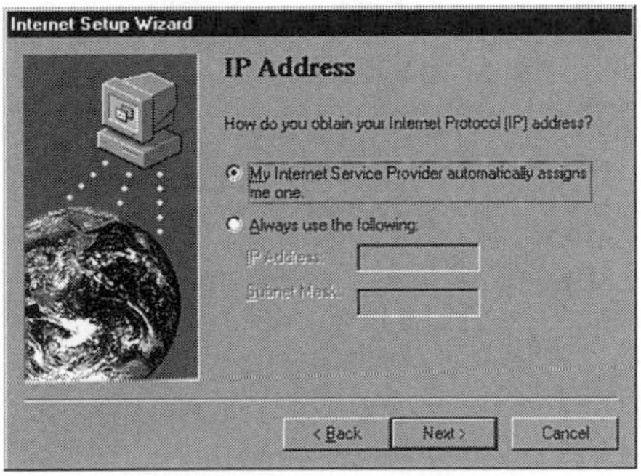

FIGURE 21.4   Supply your IP address information.

8. In the DNS Server Address dialog box, enter the IP address of your DNS (Domain Name Service) server. Your provider should supply you with this information. If your provider also supplies you with an Alternate DNS server, enter that address in the second field. Select the Next> button to continue.

9. In the Internet Mail dialog box, click the Use Internet Mail check box, and then enter your e-mail address and

the name of your mail server. (Your provider should supply you with this information.) Click the Next> button to
continue.

> **DNS (Domain Name Service)**   The means by which a
> 12-digit IP address (nnn.nnn.nnn.nnn) is converted into a
> recognizable name. (For example, the IP address of my
> service provider is 199.234.118.2; its domain name is city-
> net.com.)

10. In the Exchange Profile dialog box, enter the **Microsoft
    Exchange** profile name to use for Internet mail. Type
    the name **Internet Mail Settings**, as you see in Figure
    21.5, which is the default profile name. Click the Next>
    button to continue.

FIGURE 21.5   Set the profile name for Internet mail.

11. Finally, click the Finish button to complete your wizard
    setup. When setup is complete, the wizard creates an
    Internet icon on your desktop. You can select that icon to
    connect to the Internet through your provider.

CONNECTING TO THE INTERNET

Bear in mind that what you enter to connect to your provider
might be different than what you see in this lesson. The figures in

this lesson show my connection to my Internet provider using a Point-to-Point Protocol (PPP) connection over a 14.4 modem. Your provider should have given you the necessary information for you to log in, such as when to enter your login name (or ID) and your password, and any additional information required.

 Check the Information from Your ISP   To double-check the information you receive from your Internet provider, compare it to the list in Table 21.1. It's possible that your ISP provided you with more information than is listed in the table, but you should not have received less.

What you see here should be enough additional information to help you connect to the Internet.

1. If you purchased and Installed Microsoft Plus!, double-click the Internet icon located on your desktop. This starts the Microsoft Internet Explorer browser. The Connect To dialog box appears (see Figure 21.6).

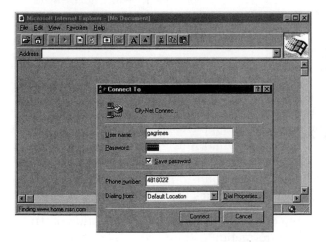

FIGURE 21.6   Connecting to your provider with MS Internet Explorer.

If you didn't purchase Microsoft Plus!, double-click the My Computer desktop icon, and then double-click the Dial-Up Networking icon. In the Dial-Up Networking dialog box, double-click the connection you created to your provider. With or without Microsoft Plus!, you should see the connection you created and the information you supplied.

2. In the Connect To dialog box, click the Connect button to dial your provider. You'll see a dialog box like the one shown in Figure 21.7.

FIGURE 21.7   This lets you know it is dialing your provider.

 My Connection Setup Didn't Dial!   If your connection setup didn't dial, your modem might not be installed correctly. Check the manual supplied by your modem manufacturer, and check the Modems configuration utility in the Control Panel.

3. If you connect to your provider, the Post-Dial Terminal Screen window now appears and prompts you to enter the information supplied by your provider (see Figure 21.8). Enter the following information as needed: login name, password, and so on. My provider had me input PPP since I use a Point-to-Point Protocol connection. When you finish, click the Continue button or press F7.

4. If your connection settings are correct and you enter the correct information required by your provider, in a few seconds, a message indicates that you are connected (see Figure 21.9). Notice that the connection keeps a clock running that shows you how long you are connected and

the speed of your connection. You may find it convenient now to close My Computer and Dial-Up Networking. Do not close the Connect To program; minimize it instead. If you close it, you exit the program and break the connection you just established.

FIGURE 21.8   The Post-Dial Terminal Screen window.

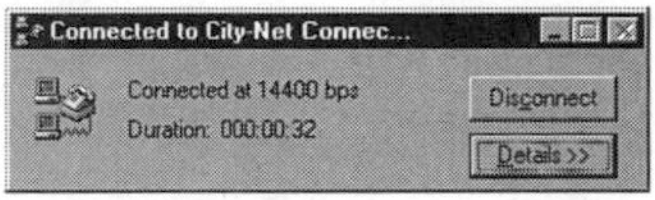

FIGURE 21.9   Your connection is complete.

TESTING YOUR CONNECTION

Before you get started browsing or experimenting with other Internet activities, test your connection with WinIPCfg—a testing utility supplied with Windows 95.

1. Click the Start button on the taskbar and choose Programs, MS-DOS Prompt to open a DOS window.

2. Type winipcfg and press Enter to run the WinIPCfg utility program. In a few seconds, the IP information you see in Figure 21.10 appears.

3. Click the More Info>> button to display Figure 21.11.

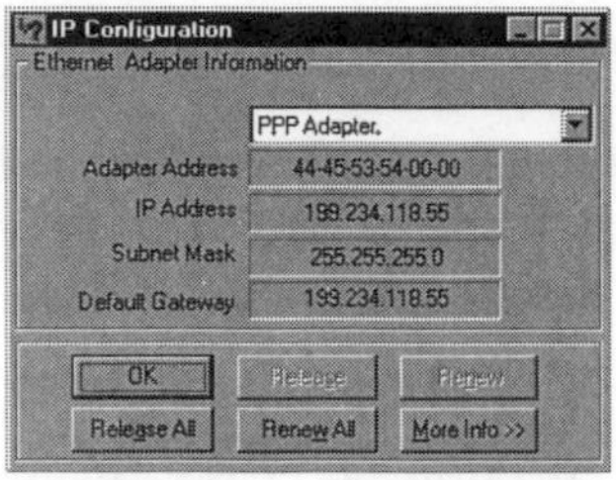

FIGURE 21.10   WinIPCfg displays IP information.

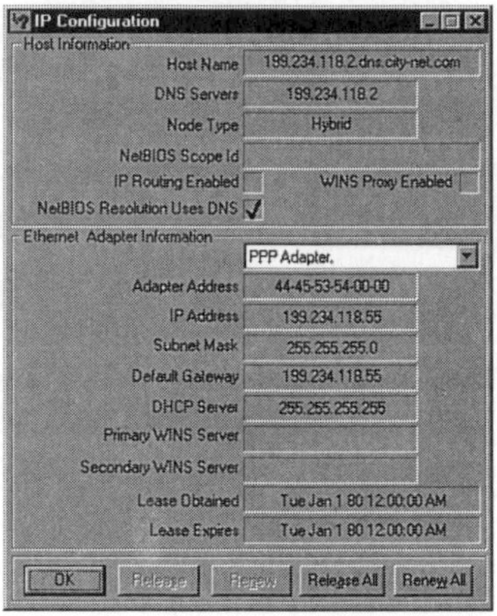

FIGURE 21.11   More information from WinIPCfg.

Most of the information displayed by WinIPCfg probably doesn't mean much to you, but the information should indicate whether you're connected to your provider (by showing your provider's name and IP address in the Host Name field, for example). The information in the IP Address field should either be your static IP address (if you set your own) or the dynamic IP address supplied by your provider. (If you didn't notice, back in the Post-Dial Terminal Screen window, your IP address was displayed.)

In this lesson, you learned how to configure your Windows 95 Internet connection, connect to your Internet service provider, and test your connection. In the next lesson, you learn how to configure an Apple Macintosh computer to connect to the Internet.

CONFIGURATION FOR MACINTOSH USERS

22

In this lesson, you'll learn about the special software you need to connect to the Internet with a Macintosh computer. You'll also learn where to get that software and how to install and configure it.

WHAT YOUR MACINTOSH NEEDS SO YOU CAN ACCESS THE INTERNET

This lesson applies to computers running Macintosh operating system 7.1 and higher. In addition to your Macintosh, modem, phone line, and account with an Internet service provider (see Lessons 2 and 18), you'll also need some special software to connect to the Internet.

Some Mac users will need MacTCP, a control panel that lets your Mac use *TCP/IP* (Transmission Control Protocol/Internet Protocol), the standard means of shuttling information around the Internet.

In addition to MacTCP, you will need MacPPP, an extension (PPP) and control panel (Config PPP) set that allows your Mac to connect to a PPP account with your service provider.

Your choice between these two extensions depends on the type of account you obtain from your Internet service provider (ISP). If you have a PPP account, you should use MacPPP.

However, if you are using Macintosh operating system 7.5.3 or higher, and you are connecting to the Internet through a PPP account, you will need different software. Operating systems 7.5.3 and higher incorporate Macintosh's Open Transport, a program that controls the way in which your computer networks. Open Transport makes it easier for you to switch from one network configuration to another: say, from your Internet connection to the AppleTalk connection for your printer, or from one Internet account to another.

If you are using Macintosh operating system 7.5.3 or higher, you will need:

- TCP/IP control panel, which is automatically installed with the operating system

- FreePPP, an extension (FreePPP) and control panel (FreePPP Setup), an efficient replacement for MacPPP

FreePPP can also be used in tandem with MacTCP on many systems in place of MacPPP.

These software configurations allow your Mac to call into your Internet service provider and connect to the Internet. Next, you'll need certain software programs that will allow you to take advantage of the resources available on the Internet.

You'll need:

- A Web browser, such as Netscape Navigator (covered in Lessons 6, 7, and 8) or Microsoft's Internet Explorer (covered in Lessons 3, 4, and 5). Both of these, and many others, are available for Macintosh.

- A file transfer protocol (FTP) utility for transferring files over the Internet (see Lesson 12). Anarchie and Fetch are excellent FTP utilities.

- An e-mail utility for sending and reading mail (see Lesson 12). Eudora is a powerful e-mail program.

- A compression utility that can reduce the size of the files you upload and download (which saves you time and money). Aladdin System's StuffIt is the Macintosh standard.

WHERE TO FIND MAC SOFTWARE

You can find the software mentioned in the preceding section, and other Internet software for your Mac, in a number of places. The following sections outline the different ways you can obtain these programs.

GET IT FROM YOUR ISP

Often, when you sign up with an Internet service provider, the ISP not only provides you with access to the Internet, but it also sends you an assortment of software to get you started. You'll probably also get instructions for configuring that software for use with your provider.

Although your service provider's starter kit might not contain the exact items I've listed, it will have an equivalent software that you can use to get connected. Once you're on the Internet, you can download and try the specific programs mentioned here, or try anything else that strikes your fancy. Check out the upcoming "Find It" section for tips on where to look for Mac software, once you're on the Internet.

BUY IT

The Internet is a hot topic, and many people want to learn about it. There are a lot of Mac-specific books available, and many of them come with software that will help you get started. This is the path of least resistance—it doesn't involve much more than a trip to the store, or a call to your favorite mail-order company.

The two best retail packages for the Mac are The Internet Starter Kit For Macintosh and The Apple Internet Connection Kit. Both are excellent choices for Mac users.

FIND IT

A lot of the software you need is available through commercial online services such as America Online and CompuServe. If you have an account with either service, you can download most of the software listed earlier, except for Netscape and Microsoft

Internet Explorer. However, the MacWeb browser available through these online services can be used until you are able to download and install Netscape or Internet Explorer.

On America Online, use the Keyword: **Net Software**, and you'll be taken to the Internet Connection's software library. There you can look for and download any of the items listed earlier in the chapter.

Using AOL Keywords Press Ctrl+K on your keyboard, and the Keyword dialog box will appear. Type in the Keyword (in this case, **Net Software**) and press Enter.

On CompuServe, use GO: FILEFINDER. In the list of file libraries, double-click the Macintosh entry. Then use File Finder to search for and download each of the items listed earlier.

GO on CompuServe Press Ctrl+G on your keyboard. The GO dialog box will appear. Type in the GO word (in this case, **FILEFINDER**) and press Enter.

If your software is set up to access the Internet, you can go to the Web sites listed below to get the latest versions of the necessary software (with the exception of MacTCP, which must be purchased, as mentioned earlier).

- MacPPP: **ftp://ftp.info.apple.com/ Apple.Support.Area/Apple.Software.Updates/US/ Macintosh/Networking-Communications/ Other_N-C/MacPPP_2.5.sea.hqx**

- FreePPP: **http://www.rockstar.com/ppp.shtml**

- Netscape Navigator: **http://home.netscape.com/try/ download/index.html**

- Microsoft Internet Explorer: **http//www.microsoft. com/ie/**

- For just about anything else in Macintosh software, try: TidBits, **ftp://ftp.tidbits.com/pub/tidbits/** or the Info_Mac archive, at **http://hyperarchive.lcs. mit.edu/HyperArchive/Abstracts/ Recent-Summary.html**

INSTALLING THE CONNECTION SOFTWARE

Once the software required for your Internet connection (MacTCP and MacPPP) has been downloaded to your computer, you'll need to install them.

> **Not So Fast!** These installation instructions are for those who downloaded the software from an online service or the Internet. If you instead bought The Internet Starter Kit for Macintosh, or Apple's Internet Connection Kit, or if you received software directly from your ISP, follow the installation and configuration instructions that came with the product.

For each component of MacTCP and MacPPP, perform the following steps:

1. Open the icon for your hard drive. Find your System Folder.

2. Open the folder that contains the item(s) you are installing. Position the folder's window so you can still see your System Folder.

3. Drag the Internet software from its window, and drop it onto your System Folder icon. (MacTCP will have one control panel. MacPPP will have both an extension and control panel. FreePPP has two control panels and one extension.)

4. Your computer will ask if it's okay to put each item where it belongs—in the Extensions folder, and/or the Control Panels folder. Click OK.

5. Restart your Mac (select the Special menu, and choose Restart) to enable your Mac to use the software you've installed.

When you're done, MacTCP ends in the Control Panels folder.

If you're using MacPPP, the PPP extension will be found in your Extensions folder, and Config PPP will appear in your Control Panels folder. If you are using FreePPP, the FreePPP extension will be found in your Extensions folder, and FreePPP Setup and ~FreePPP Menu will be found in your Control Panels folder.

CONFIGURING YOUR SOFTWARE

You need to provide your Internet software with information about your Internet service provider. You get that information directly from your ISP, usually in a manual or on an information sheet. Don't try to configure your connection software until you have this information in your hands.

MacTCP

To configure MacTCP, follow these steps:

1. Select the Control Panels folder and double-click the MacTCP icon. The MacTCP control panel opens; it will look something like Figure 22.1.

2. Click the **PPP** icon in the top section of the Control Panel to select it (see Figure 22.1), and then click More. The configuration dialog box shown in Figure 22.2 appears.

3. Carefully enter the information you've received from your ISP. Generally, you'll need to select one of the options in the Obtain Address box (located in the upper-left

corner of Figure 22.2). Then, in the Domain Name Server Information box in the lower-right corner, you'll fill in the first line under DOMAIN and IP ADDRESS. Because no two ISPs are alike, follow exactly the directions you have received from your ISP.

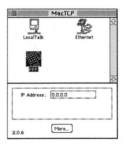

FIGURE 22.1   The MacTCP Control Panel.

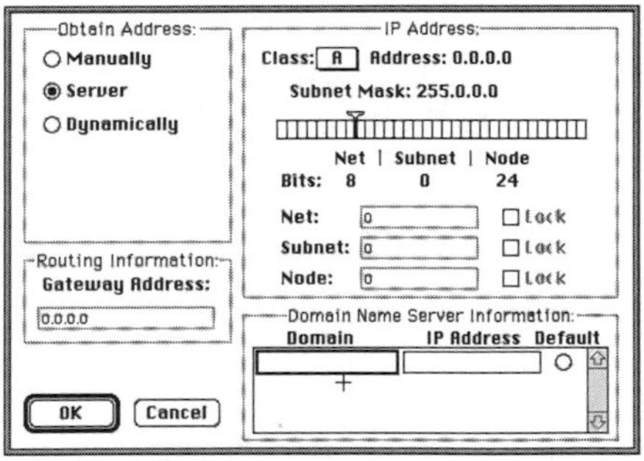

FIGURE 22.2   The MacTCP configuration options.

4. When you finish entering the information, click OK to save it. Then close the MacTCP Control Panel.

5. Your Mac may ask you to restart the computer, so that the changes you've made can take effect. Open the Special menu and select Restart.

MacPPP

Follow these steps to configure MacPPP:

1. Select the Control Panels folder (if necessary), and double-click the Config PPP icon. Config PPP will open, and it will look something like Figure 22.3.

FIGURE 22.3 The Config PPP Control Panel.

2. From the Port Name pull-down box near the top of the control panel, select the port to which your modem is connected.

3. Click the Config button in the lower-left corner of the Control Panel, and the dialog box shown in Figure 22.4 will appear.

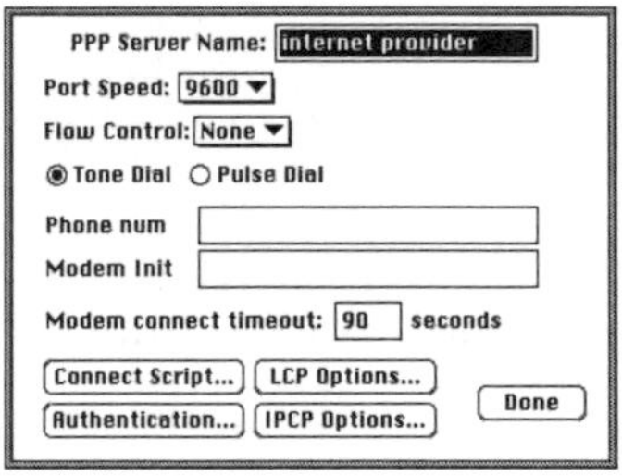

FIGURE 22.4 The Config PPP Control Panel.

4. Type the name of your ISP into the PPP Server Name box at the top of the Control Panel.

5. Next, select a speed from the Port Speed pull-down box. Use the setting that is one step above the speed of your modem.

6. Click the button for the type of phone line you have: Tone Dial, or Pulse Dial.

7. Type your ISP's access telephone number in the Phone num box.

8. In the remaining boxes, enter any additional information your ISP may have given you, if any.

9. You may or may not need to configure the Connect Script, Authentication, LCP Options, or IPCP Options, depending on your ISP's particular needs. If you do, carefully follow their instructions.

10. When you finish, click Done and close the Config PPP Control Panel.

Notice that the PPP Server text box now shows the name of your ISP. That's why the text box in Figure 22.3 said "internet provider"; my connection had already been configured.

FreePPP

Follow these steps to configure FreePPP:

1. Open the FreePPP Setup Control Panel (see Figure 22.5).

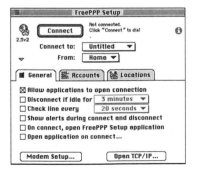

FIGURE 22.5   The FreePPP Setup Control Panel.

2. Click the Accounts tab in the middle of the panel, and then click New (see Figure 22.6).

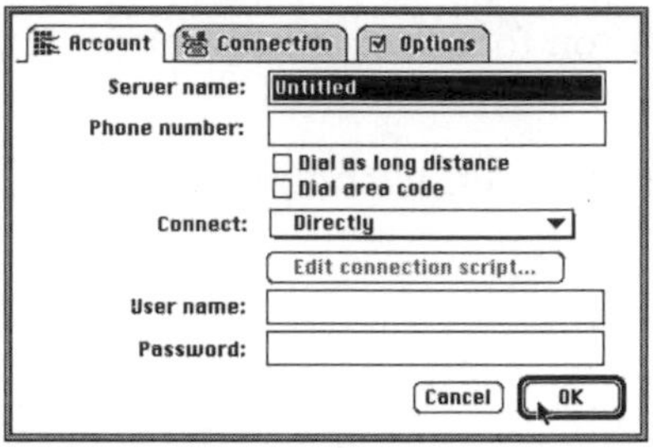

FIGURE 22.6   The FreePPP Account tab.

3. Type the name of your ISP in the Server Name box. In the Phone number box, type in the correct telephone number you will use to connect to your ISP. In the Connect pull-down box, choose how you will connect to the Internet (probably Directly), and type your username and connecting password into the appropriate spaces.

4. Open both the Connection and Options tabs, and type in the correct information, as given to you by your ISP.

5. Click OK, and return to the FreePPP Setup Control Panel. Click Open TCP/IP to reveal the TCP/IP Control Panel.

TCP/IP

Follow these steps to configure TCP/IP:

1. If you have not yet opened the TCP/IP Control Panel (shown in Figure 22.7), then do so.

2. Select your manner of connection in the Connect via pull-down box (probably FreePPP).

3. Make a selection in the Configure pull-down box (probably Using PPP Server).

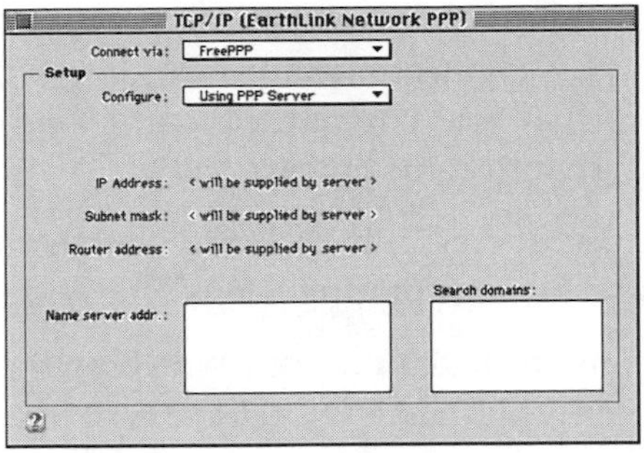

FIGURE 22.7   The TCP/IP control panel.

4. If the Name server addr and Search domains boxes are blank, fill them in using the information you have obtained from your ISP.

5. Close the **TCP/IP** Control Panel. Close the **FreePPP Setup** Control Panel.

YOUR OTHER INTERNET APPLICATIONS

Your Web browser, your e-mail utility, and any other applications you want to use on the Internet will also require information about your ISP (such as the name of the mail server, the news server, and so on). This information should be provided by your ISP in a manual or information sheet. The applications' Help files will explain which information will be needed, and where it should be placed.

CONNECTING TO YOUR ISP

After you configure your software, test out the configuration by connecting to your ISP. Follow these steps:

1. Open **Config PPP**, **FreePPP Setup**, (whichever one you're using) as described in the appropriate configuration section.

2. Click Open (in Config PPP), or Connect (in FreePPP and in InterSLIP). A connection status window will open, telling you what your computer is doing as it goes through the connection process.

3. If you connect successfully, you can launch your Web browser, and begin exploring the World Wide Web.

4. When you're finished, quit your Web browser and any other Internet applications you have running.

5. Click Close (in Config PPP) or Disconnect (in FreePPP) to sign off from your ISP.

If by some chance you are not able to connect to your ISP, retrace your steps through the configuration process. Make sure you've entered the information from your ISP accurately (a mistake in a series of numbers is the most common problem), and try again. If you double-check your ISP information and it seems correct, you might want to give your ISP's technical support number a call. Ask for its Macintosh person, and see if he or she can help you out.

In this lesson, you learned to connect to the Internet with your Macintosh. In the next lesson, you learn how access the Internet with an Online service such as America Online or The Microsoft Network.

ACCESSING THE INTERNET WITH AN ONLINE SERVICE

In this lesson, you learn how to access the World Wide Web using two of the major online services: AOL and The Microsoft Network.

AMERICA ONLINE

America Online, usually just referred to as AOL, is currently the largest of the major online services with a reported user base of more than 10 million. If you've bought a computer magazine in the last six months, chances are you already have AOL software since many computers now have AOL software pre-installed. The major online services have all been feverishly distributing their disks and CD-ROMs attached to virtually any and every computer magazine that has anything to say about the Internet. The Internet has been the hot computer topic during the last year and all of the online services are trying to cash in on this ground swell. During the past year, all of the major online services have added Internet access to their list of services.

If you haven't picked up a computer magazine lately, you can call AOL at (800)827-3338 and order its software.

INSTALLING AND SETTING UP AOL

AOL is only available on the Windows and Mac platforms. In this lesson, you will be demonstrating AOL on a Windows 95 platform. AOL is not particular about running on either Windows 3.1, 95, or NT, and none of the three flavors of Windows has an advantage when running AOL.

To install AOL, follow these steps:

1. Place your AOL disk into your drive (floppy disk or CD) and select the File, Run command.

2. At the Run prompt, type **x:\setup**, where *x* is the drive you placed the disk in.

3. Follow the prompts to complete the installation.

Double-click the AOL icon to start the program. When you start AOL the first time, you will have to sign up for the service. Follow the prompts to sign up for AOL. The setup will take approximately 3–5 minutes.

When you complete the setup, follow the prompts to the Main Menu shown in Figure 23.1.

FIGURE 23.1   AOL's Main Menu.

From the Main Menu, click Internet Connection to proceed to AOL's gateway to the Internet (see Figure 23.2).

In the Internet Connection window, click the World Wide Web icon to start AOL's Web browser. Figure 23.3 shows the opening screen you will see.

AOL's Web browser works much the same as Netscape and MS Internet Explorer. You enter the URL of the Web page or site you want to visit and in a few seconds, the page appears on your screen. For example, to visit the Smithsonian Web site, you can enter **http://www.si.edu/**, and in a few seconds, you're at the Smithsonian's Web site (see Figure 23.4).

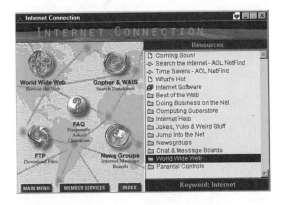

Figure 23.2   AOL's Internet Connection.

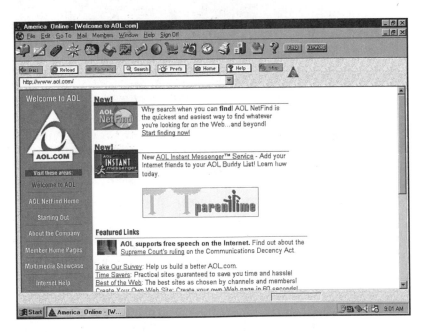

Figure 23.3   AOL's Web browser.

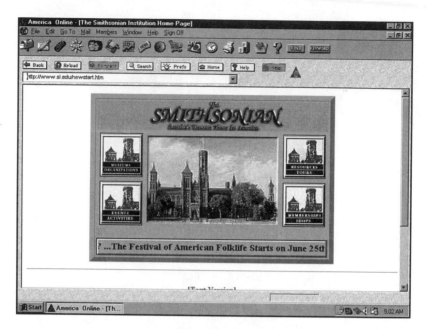

FIGURE 23.4   Visit the Smithsonian online.

THE MICROSOFT NETWORK

The inclusion of software for the Microsoft Network with Windows 95 caused a protracted legal battle between Microsoft and several of the major online service companies. They lost, Microsoft won, and your MSN software is bundled with Windows 95. This also partly explains the flurry of free software from the other services "bundled" with practically every PC Magazine in the past two years.

The upside for Microsoft with bundling MSN software in Windows 95 is that you do not have to get another disk or order a software installation package in order to install MSN. The downside for Microsoft is that MSN is only available for Windows 95. Therefore, if you're not running Windows 95, or are not thinking about switching to Windows 95, you can bypass this section.

If you are running Windows 95 and you did not install MSN when you installed Windows 95, adding MSN is a snap. Follow these steps:

1. Open the Windows 95 Control Panel and click Add/Re-move Programs.

> **There is No Listing for Microsoft Network**   If you don't see MSN in the Add/Remove listing, you can still install MSN using the Internet Setup Wizard by selecting MSN as your service provider.

2. Select the Windows Setup tab in the Add/Remove Pro-grams Properties dialog box. Select the check box next to The Microsoft Network and click OK.

3. Follow the prompts to install The Microsoft Network. Make sure you have your Windows 95 installation CD or disks handy. You will be prompted to insert them so the installation program can copy the appropriate files to your PC.

4. When the installation is completed, you should see a new icon on your desktop for The Microsoft Network. Double-click the MSN icon to start the program.

5. Follow the initial sign-on prompts until you see the main menu pictured in Figure 23.5.

6. Click United States to access the English language section or the language you would prefer to use.

7. In a few seconds, MS Internet Explorer appears, displaying the MSN Home Page located at **www.msn.com** (see Figure 23.6).

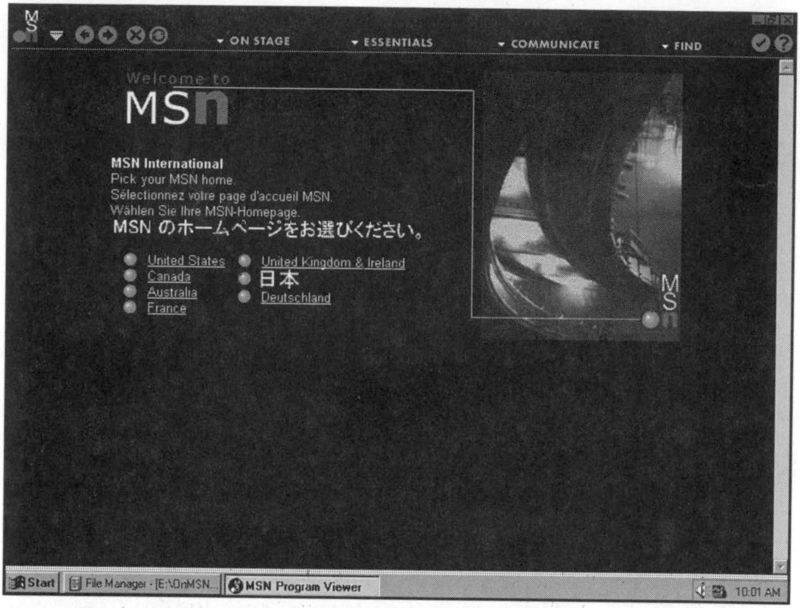

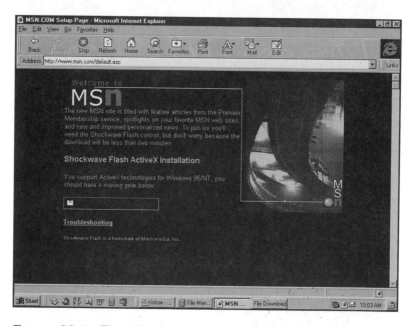

FIGURE 23.5   MSN's Main Menu.

FIGURE 23.6   The MSN home page.

INDEX

Complete and Return this Card
for a *FREE* Computer Book Catalog

Thank you for purchasing this book! You have purchased a superior computer book written expressly for your needs. To continue to provide the kind of up-to-date, pertinent coverage you've come to expect from us, we need to hear from you. Please take a minute to complete and return this self-addressed, postage-paid form. In return, we'll send you a free catalog of all our computer books on topics ranging from word processing to programming and the internet.

Mr. ☐   Mrs. ☐   Ms. ☐   Dr. ☐

Name (first) ☐☐☐☐☐☐☐☐☐ (M.I.) ☐ (last) ☐☐☐☐☐☐☐☐☐☐☐☐

Address ☐☐☐☐☐☐☐☐☐☐☐☐☐☐☐☐☐☐☐☐☐

☐☐☐☐☐☐☐☐☐☐☐☐☐☐☐☐☐☐☐☐☐

City ☐☐☐☐☐☐☐☐☐☐☐☐ State ☐☐ Zip ☐☐☐☐☐ ☐☐☐☐

Phone ☐☐☐ ☐☐☐ ☐☐☐☐   Fax ☐☐☐ ☐☐☐ ☐☐☐☐

Company Name ☐☐☐☐☐☐☐☐☐☐☐☐☐☐☐☐

E-mail address ☐☐☐☐☐☐☐☐☐☐☐☐☐☐☐☐☐☐☐☐☐

1. Please check at least (3) influencing factors for purchasing this book.

Front or back cover information on book .... ☐
Special approach to the content .... ☐
Completeness of content .... ☐
Author's reputation .... ☐
Publisher's reputation .... ☐
Book cover design or layout .... ☐
Index or table of contents of book .... ☐
Price of book .... ☐
Special effects, graphics, illustrations .... ☐
Other (Please specify): _____ ☐

2. How did you first learn about this book?

Internet Site .... ☐
Saw in Macmillan Computer
    Publishing catalog .... ☐
Recommended by store personnel .... ☐
Saw the book on bookshelf at store .... ☐
Recommended by a friend .... ☐
Received advertisement in the mail .... ☐
Saw an advertisement in: _____ ☐
Read book review in: _____ ☐
Other (Please specify): _____ ☐

3. How many computer books have you purchased in the last six months?

This book only .... ☐   3 to 5 books .... ☐
2 books .... ☐   More than 5 .... ☐

4. Where did you purchase this book?

Bookstore .... ☐
Computer Store .... ☐
Consumer Electronics Store .... ☐
Department Store .... ☐
Office Club .... ☐
Warehouse Club .... ☐
Mail Order .... ☐
Direct from Publisher .... ☐
Internet site .... ☐
Other (Please specify): .... ☐

5. How long have you been using a computer?

Less than 6 months .. ☐   6 months to a year ..... ☐
1 to 3 years .... ☐   More than 3 years ...... ☐

6. What is your level of experience with personal computers and with the subject of this book?

	With PCs	With subject of book
New	☐	☐
Casual	☐	☐
Accomplished	☐	☐
Expert	☐	☐

Source Code — ISBN: 0-7897-1405-1

7. Which of the following best describes your job title?

Administrative Assistant ☐
Coordinator ☐
Manager/Supervisor ☐
Director ☐
Vice President ☐
President/CEO/COO ☐
Lawyer/Doctor/Medical Professional ☐
Teacher/Educator/Trainer ☐
Engineer/Technician ☐
Consultant ☐
Not employed/Student/Retired ☐
Other (Please specify): ☐

8. Which of the following best describes the area of the company your job title falls under?

Accounting ☐
Engineering ☐
Manufacturing ☐
Marketing ☐
Operations ☐
Sales ☐
Other (Please specify): ☐

9. What is your age?

Under 20 ☐
21-29 ☐
30-39 ☐
40-49 ☐
50-59 ☐
60-over ☐

10. Are you:

Male ☐
Female ☐

11. Which computer publications do you read regularly? (Please list)

_____
_____
_____
_____
_____
_____
_____
_____
_____
_____

Comments: _____
_____
_____

Fold here and scotch-tape to mail